HELP YOUR SELF

HELP
YOUR
SELF

*Today's Obsession
with Satan's Oldest Lie*

STEPHANIE FORBES

CROSSWAY BOOKS • WHEATON, ILLINOIS
A DIVISION OF GOOD NEWS PUBLISHERS

Help Your Self

Published by Crossway Books
    A division of Good News Publishers
    1300 Crescent Street
    Wheaton, Illinois 60187

Cover illustration: Keith Stubblefield

Cover design: Cindy Kiple

Manuscript editing: Leonard G. Goss and Lila Bishop

First printing, 1996

Printed in the United States of America

Library of Congress Cataloging-in-Publication Data
Forbes, Stephanie L., 1950-
    Help your self : today's obsession with Satan's oldest lie.
      p.   cm.
    Includes bibliographical references (p.   ) and index.
    ISBN 0-89107-902-5
    1. Theology, Doctrinal 2. Self-worship--Controversial
literature. 3. Christian life. 4. Deception. 5. Self-help
techniques. I. Title.
BT78.F54   1996
248—dc20   96-12499

05		04		03		02		01		00		99		98		97		96
15	14	13	12	11	10	9	8	7	6	5	4	3	2	1

To my mother,
who taught me to read dictionaries
to learn about words
and the Bible to learn about myself

Contents

Preface

People write books for all sorts of reasons. Some writers will tell you that the idea for a story or a work of nonfiction banged around on the inside of their heads so forcefully that they had no choice but to write the book. It was write or go mad. Up to now, I would have said that writers of that ilk must have unusually soft skulls. But then, up to now, my work has been mostly at the behest of other people and expressed only their ideas or research or programs.

My opinion of the "compulsion" theory of writing began to change when I was asked to ghostwrite a book on personal success. For various reasons, the project fell through. But it left me with, in words every *Star Wars* fan will recognize, *a very bad feeling.* That feeling, I realized when I analyzed it, arose from a fundamental conflict between the success message I had been asked to promulgate and my basic Christian beliefs.

But the very bad feeling was only the beginning. I began to notice success and other self-help messages everywhere I went. I couldn't walk past a bookstore without seeing prominent displays of Og Mandino's or Tony Robbins's or John Bradshaw's latest expressions of self-help. I couldn't turn on public television without seeing Depak Chopra expounding his spiritual success laws or Leo Buscaglia lecturing on self-love. Commercial television seemed always to be airing some program or other on happiness or personal fulfillment or self-esteem or recovery. Maria Shriver was looking at the psychological aspects of personal contentment. John Stossel was taking a more scientific approach, reporting on the neurochemical aspects of happiness.

Embedded in all the self-help messages I saw around me was the tacit assumption that human beings can and should seek their own fulfillment on their own terms. This assumption, I was realizing more and more, has been affecting and is being expressed by every aspect of American culture, from entertainment to education to scientific inquiry to health care to public policy.

Worst of all, this anti-Christian assumption has been making serious inroads into American Christianity. And very few people (or so it seemed to me) appeared to notice.

So you see, much as I hate to admit it, I felt compelled to write this book. But just writing a book isn't enough. Unless someone reads what you've written, the uneasy feeling, the compulsion to express your ideas, doesn't go away. So I am extremely grateful to Crossway Books for helping to rid me of that frightful banging inside my head. But I am even more grateful to the Holy Spirit for putting the hammer there in the first place.

PART I

Understanding the Self-Help Movement

1

What Is Self-Help?
A Bird's-eye View

I t's the third Monday night of the month, and the planning com-
mittees of First Church are hard at work on new programs for
the fall. In the library the adult Christian education committee
sits around a table piled with the numerous books and manuals
under consideration—a book on building self-esteem in your mate,
a course on financial planning, a workbook on discovering personal
significance, a manual on drugs used in psychotherapy, a book on
avoiding negative relationships, a course on learning how to say no
and set personal boundaries, and a study guide on journaling. One
woman timidly suggests that they offer a course on the theology and
apologetics of Francis Schaeffer, but someone quickly dismisses her
proposal as irrelevant to the needs of modern seeker-members.

In the choir room, the worship committee studies the goals
for the Sunday morning "program." Everyone agrees that the
worship experience needs to be more personal. "We need to get
these people excited," says the music minister. "They should leave
here feeling really wowed by our presentation."

"Yeah, and they should feel really good about themselves for
coming. I mean, if they don't feel something personal, we've
failed, right?" says the committee chair.

"I think it's also a question of numbers," says another committee member. "We have to be practical here. We're in competition with a lot of other stuff that's really a lot more interesting. Face it, we've got to give them something that they'll want to come back for. That old boring church service just doesn't work anymore." Everyone nods in agreement.

Down the hall, the women's ministry steering group adjourns early and heads for the associate pastor's office for week five of a thirteen-week anger workshop. The husbands and significant others of workshop participants are meeting in the basement fellowship hall to discuss ways for getting in touch with their feminine side.

The singles' ministry committee is having a lively debate about new weight-training and aerobics classes. The argument centers on how to deal with people who might develop an exercise addiction. "Maybe we should start a kind of twelve-step prevention program. I know I could really use something like that to keep me focused on what's important for me," suggests a trim coed. "We could even include friends of participants, who might become codependents. It would be a really positive way to get more people into church." A quick vote ratifies her suggestion, and the chair appoints a new committee to develop the program.

Scenes very much like these are being acted out in churches of all denominations all over the United States. What is happening? American Christians, bombarded by secular messages of personal success and fulfillment and self-esteem and happiness, have begun to embrace the modern movement known as self-help, a movement already remaking Christianity in the image of man, a movement based on Satan's oldest lie—that we can be like God. Obsessed with the desire to put ourselves in God's place, our secular culture has substituted dysfunction for sin, feeling good for being good, self-esteem for shame, and success for sacrifice. Christians, seduced by the promises of self-help, are using God as a form of personal validation and comfort rather than worshiping Him as Creator, Judge, and Redeemer. As Christians we need to recognize Satan's lie in self-help and firmly reject its teachings for ourselves individually and for the body of Christ collectively. We need to stand firm with the authoritative Word of God and orthodox Christian theology against Satan's latest and perhaps most subtle attack in his campaign for the souls of men and women. At stake is no less than our acknowledgment of God's sovereignty, our radical discipleship to Jesus Christ, and our witness to a fallen world.

To arm ourselves against self-help's message, we first need to understand what self-help is. Let me make it clear that by self-help I do not mean "do-it-yourself." The do-it-yourself book is a staple on my bookshelf. Because I have neither the time nor the patience to take technical classes, I rely on do-it-yourself books to teach me all sorts of useful skills. With the help of do-it-yourself books, I have learned to knit, crochet, quilt, refinish furniture, grow vegetables, design perennial gardens, lay ceramic tile, and hang wallpaper. My husband and I have referred to these books to help us add a deck to our house, remodel a kitchen, make plumbing repairs, install circuit breakers, and build bookshelves. Next to a good Bible concordance, dictionary, and thesaurus, do-it-yourself books are my favorite reference works.

Self-help is a far cry from do-it-yourself. The focus of the do-it-yourself book is a project or skill to master—tax-exempt investment strategies or home canning or conversational Italian. The project of the self-help book is always *me*. And this is where self-help is such a danger for Christians. When Christ calls us to discipleship, He bids us come and die, die to the self so completely that even the act of self-denial is a sin when we think about the self we are denying and not solely about Christ. Peter could answer Christ's call to walk on water as long as he kept his eyes on Christ. When he looked down and realized what he was doing, he sank. So it is with us.

Whatever else they may stress, all self-help materials have in common a total and relentless focus on the self. Even when other people are taken into consideration in self-help strategies, their presence is important only insofar as it affects the self. Some self-help books, for example, recommend altruistic behavior because helping other people makes one feel useful and good about the self. Other self-help works provide advice on forging strong relationships because interpersonal ties help one fulfill the self. Always and in every way, these books lead us back to the self.

Self-help tells me that it is my human birthright to be the center of my own universe. I have the right to my feelings and their full expression. I have the right to pursue my heart's desires. I have the right to love myself. I have the right to do what I want, be what I want, accumulate what I want. Self-help tells me that putting myself first is healthy; sacrificing myself to any person or any cause is unhealthy. To be fully human is to be fully me, to be full of me. The justification for all this self-ness? I AM my own justification.

The message of self-help is heady stuff. It is the same message the serpent used to tempt Eve when he told her that she could be like God. The serpent today may be dressed in the new scales of self-help, but it is the same old serpent and the same old message. Eve couldn't resist it; neither can we, judging from the phenomenal success of self-help books, audio and video tapes, and workshops.

The popularity and acceptance of self-help materials and the positions of power held by self-help "experts" were alarmingly illustrated in a recent issue of *Newsweek*, which reported that President Clinton is consulting Anthony Robbins and Stephen Covey, two entrepreneurs who have turned the public's hunger for personal success and fulfillment into enormous business empires. According to that same article, House Speaker Newt Gingrich is a serious devotee of Covey, whose message is no more than a secular version of his Mormon beliefs.[1] Both as Christians and as American citizens, we need to understand what and who our country's leaders are consulting for advice that may well shape public policy.

TYPES OF SELF-HELP

Self-help materials can be divided into several different categories, depending upon one's definition and focus. I have identified what I believe to be six major groups. Like any categories devised by man, my divisions are somewhat arbitrary, and there is some overlap between groups. Nevertheless, I think that these groups include all the major types of self-help material and provide some indication of the scope of this genre. The examples provided in each category are of books, although video and audio tapes, lectures, and seminars also exist for each group.

While my intent is to describe the features of these self-help categories, you will undoubtedly notice that I tend to focus on their shortcomings. This is not to say that these books have no redeeming features. Some, such as certain books on self-healing, can be very useful, as when they advocate more healthful eating and provide sample diets that prove useful for people undergoing chemotherapy for cancer. The nuts-and-bolts books and programs, which are really versions of how-to materials, are not my primary focus, although I readily acknowledge that there is some overlap between how-to and self-help in certain categories. You really need to understand the difference so you can arm yourself against the propaganda preached by the self-help books that are fast becoming the scriptures of an American secular religion.

1. Recovery

This category of self-help includes material designed for people recovering from a host of traumatic experiences, inappropriate behaviors, addictions, or just plain unhappiness. Since just about any behavior or past experience can be interpreted as an addiction or a stumbling block to effective living, most Americans can be seen as a potential market for recovery material. And when you add to this market all the relatives and friends of addicted or dysfunctional people, for whom recovery material and support groups also exist, you've pretty much bagged the entire population.

Most recovery material today uses some variation on the twelve-step program pioneered by Alcoholics Anonymous. Unlike AA, the use of these steps goes far beyond treatment for a drug dependency. Addicts, recovery material insists, can suffer from more than substance abuse. They may be addicted to harmful behaviors or poor judgment or uncontrolled emotions. Chronic lateness, shopping, exercise, work, sex, gambling, anger, eating, sleeping, reading, TV watching, and even religion have all been identified as problems from which people need to recover. In fact, for just about any activity, you can find those who claim to be addicted to it and others who have written books about it, either as experts in treating the addiction or as recovering or recovered addicts sharing their stories to help those with similar addictions.

Typical of recovery books is *Belonging: Bonds of Healing & Recovery*. This general book describes addiction and its causes and lists the twelve steps of recovery and how to use them. One of the book's authors confesses that while he personally suffers from no substance addiction and did not grow up in an alcoholic home, he still recommends the twelve-step program for everyone who wants to be happy and live effectively. The book encourages readers to be part of a healing community whether or not they have anything to be healed of. The belonging is the goal.

Another such book is *The 12 Stages of Healing*. (Once again, twelve is the magic number.) Written by a chiropractor, this book encourages the reader to fully experience each stage before moving on to the next. Eventually, you are able to enter a healed or healing community.

2. Success

Books on achieving personal, career, and material success are probably the oldest type of self-help literature and continue to be one of the biggest sellers. While their focus may not be as blatantly acquisitive as the books of the 1980s, the 1990s' success books continue to stress that we both deserve and are able to have everything we ever wanted in life. Of course, today's books also emphasize that it is not enough to be rich, powerful, and successful in our careers. We must also be fulfilled in all other areas of our lives—our relationships, our family ties, our recreational activities, our spiritual expressions. The word often used to describe this well-rounded life is *balanced,* which is the success writer's version of the recovery term *centered.*

I could spend (or waste) pages and pages providing examples of success books. My local library includes 252 books under this listing in its computerized card catalog. A fairly recent and typical example of the genre is *I Could Do Anything If I Only Knew What It Was.* Written by one of the many success gurus, this book tells you how to discover what you really want out of life so that you can feel happy and successful.

Under this umbrella category of success, I also include books and programs on positive thinking, positive self-talk, optimism, making friends, and personal improvement. This last type of self-help book, covering topics such as diet, exercise, dressing, and grooming, is really concerned with personal power, happiness, fulfillment, and success. The skills being taught serve only as a means to that end. One such book is the bestseller on dieting (or on not dieting, but still being thin, fit, and happy), *Stop the Insanity.*

3. Self-Esteem

Of all self-help categories, self-esteem is probably the most blatantly "me" oriented. According to self-esteem materials, self-love is the first and highest calling of human beings; it can be sacrificed to nothing and to no one. Success books, by contrast, may help you become a better entrepreneur, which, let's face it, is good for America's economy. And recovery books aim to put you back on your feet so you can contribute to society and get along in your community. But self-esteem books keep you focused primarily on your relationship with yourself, even when they advocate what in other contexts might be considered "moral" behavior.

Self-esteem materials often introduce strategies common in other self-help programs, tactics such as positive mental attitude, imaging, affirmation therapy, and journaling. But the goal of these strategies is always ego enhancement.

Two popular examples of self-esteem books are *The Six Pillars of Self Esteem*, by psychologist Nathaniel Branden, and Gloria Steinem's trip down memory lane, *Revolution from Within: A Book of Self-Esteem*. Both of these books assume that self-esteem is the most important aspiration of human beings, that it can be learned, and that it is life-transforming.

4. Affirmations

Affirmation books may be best described as compendiums of banal sayings that operate ostensibly to uplift the reader and help him face each day with a positive thought about himself. Usually small (about four by six inches in size) and brightly colored, these little books are perennially hot sellers. According to some analysts, the market for these books is second only to that for the Bible.[2] Readers of these books (one might in truth call them devotees) seem to use them in much the same way that Christians use and take comfort and courage from *Our Daily Bread*.

Affirmation books are typically written by people who choose not to reveal their full names, for reasons that remain unclear to me. (I assume it has nothing to do with simple embarrassment about the inferior writing of superficial sentiment.) One writer, for example, identifies herself only as the author of *Each Day a New Beginning*. Perhaps such writers, like The Artist Formerly Known as Prince, see their names as part of the paternalistic society that victimized them before they entered recovery. *Embracing the Journey*, written by a recovering sexual abuse victim who identifies herself only as Nancy W., is typical of the affirmation book style. (It is also typical in that it is written by someone "in recovery.") Each page offers a brief, positive statement, such as: "I am standing up for my beliefs," followed by a short essay with an explanation and personal example.

5. Inspiration

Inspirational books, tapes, lectures, and seminars seem to fill the need of many people for regular doses of encouragement—pep talks, if you will. Revival meetings serve much the same function for some evangelical and fundamentalist Christians. As well as providing encouragement, these materials stimulate personal change and direct life choices by offering advice for a more fulfilling life, a more connected life, a more life-filled life, sometimes just a more human life or a more personal life. More than the other types of self-help literature, inspirational materials are primarily spiritual in tone, provide lots of personal anecdotes, and make the reader feel good. "Heart-warming" is the term that comes to mind when describing inspirational literature. In a television interview, inspirational author Jack Canfield said that his book offers hope, love, and self-esteem for sale.[3] Apparently, puppies aren't the only love money can buy.

Inspirational literature includes books such as Scott Peck's *The Road Less Traveled*, Norman Vincent Peale's *The Power of Positive Thinking*, Leo Buscaglia's *Loving*, and *Chicken Soup for the Soul* by Jack Canfield and Mark Victor Hansen. Judging from the phenomenal sales of these books, the authors have tapped a deep longing in Americans to feel good about human beings in general and themselves in particular.

6. Self-Healing

This category of self-help includes books that purport to tell readers how to gain control of their bodies and their states of health. Some of these books are quite specific and deal with particular diseases, such as cancer or heart disease or arthritis. Others are more general and deal with overall health and physical and mental wellbeing. The implication of these books is that physical health is the result of some psychic or spiritual body awareness, attitude, or miraculous intervention that is generally nonspecific and impersonal—more like a life force than a supernatural being with intelligence and purpose.

Perhaps the best known of the self-healing books is Dr. Bernie S. Siegel's *Love, Medicine & Miracles*. In books such as Siegel's, even death is interpreted as a miracle, as long as the patient has the right attitude about it. Absent from all of these books is the Christian position that illness, suffering, and death resulted from man's fall and that creation will not be relieved of this burden until Christ establishes His eternal kingdom.

FEATURES OF SELF-HELP

All self-help materials, regardless of their major thrust, share certain features. Of course, some features may be more characteristic of one type of self-help than another. Inspirational books, for example, tend to be more spiritual than success books, which are more pragmatic than affirmation books. Nevertheless, all self-help materials demonstrate the following attributes to some degree.

Failure to engage the intellect

Historian Richard Hofstadter has observed that intelligence and intellect are not one and the same thing. While animals may exhibit intelligence, only man is blessed with intellect. The intellect, according to Hofstadter, uniquely manifests human dignity.

It "examines, ponders, wonders, theorizes, criticizes, imagines." It "evaluates evaluations."[4] This is exactly what the self-help movement seeks to avoid.

Anti-intellectualism is, for me, one of the most disturbing elements of self-help materials. These materials provide advice and "information" that cannot stand up to any rigorous scientific test, historical evaluation, or philosophical scrutiny. The critical mind is a liability to self-help because it asks uncomfortable questions and looks for sense, order, and rationality.

A perfect example of the anti-intellectualism of self-help/inspirational books is Robert Fulghum's major bestseller, *All I Really Need to Know I Learned in Kindergarten.* I remember kindergarten clearly, and I can think of nothing about it that stimulated the mind, engaged the intellect, encouraged critical thought, or rewarded independent thinking. In fact, the major goal of kindergarten, according to an educator I spoke with many years ago when my children were in preschool, is primarily socialization. Kindergarten is the ultimate outcome-based educational experience. It teaches children how to get along in a group, how to wait their turn, how to share, how to stand in line, how to follow instructions. Yes, these are all useful skills, but they do nothing to excite the intellect or contribute to our common body of knowledge.

In fact, a good case can be made for the belief that these skills stifle the creativity and intellectual inquiry necessary to advance learning. Certainly, a child does not become an artist by mastering the skill of coloring within the lines of a picture that someone else has drawn. Tracing letters of the alphabet, memorizing songs, or sitting quietly listening to little golden books does not make writers or musicians, poets or philosophers, theologians or scientists.

Self-help writers recognize that most people are looking for easy answers, simple formulas, and money-back guarantees to solve their problems. Most people feel uncomfortable with open-ended questions and even more uncomfortable with intellectuals.

Warnings against the intellectual elite are part and parcel of not only our secular but also our religious, especially evangelical, culture. (For a full discussion of anti-intellectualism in American evangelicalism, I encourage you to read Mark Noll's *The Scandal of the Evangelical Mind* and Os Guinness's *Fit Bodies, Fat Minds*.) Inquiry and speculation are not only not encouraged, but are actually decried by self-help writers. "If you believe you can, you can," say these writers, flying in the face of practical wisdom and reason. And small support groups, the mainstay of many types of self-help, exist not to challenge people, but to provide comfort in a community setting, according to Robert Wuthnow, professor of sociology at Princeton University.[5]

The illogic of self-help really struck home recently when I was working on another project and came into contact with a success "coach." This coach teaches that it is possible to have or become or do anything you want, as long as you know *what* it is you want and *why* you want it. (Yes, you also have to buy his books and tapes and practice his system for success.) My conversation with the success guru went something like this:

"I don't understand how your system works."

"First of all, tell me what you'd do if you could do anything in the world. Your ideal career."

"Well, I've always wanted to be a great opera diva. Maybe like Elly Ameling or Kathleen Battle."

"Okay, that's your goal. Now we just need to figure out how you can achieve it—you know, the work and study you'll need to do, that sort of thing."

"To begin with, I'd need to be born with a whole new set of physical equipment. I'll be honest with you—I just don't have the pipes for opera. No matter how much I want it or how much I study, I'll never sing with the Met. So how can your success program help me get what I want?"

"Let me tell you a little story," he said. "This is a true story. I had a client who had always wanted to sing in the Mormon Tabernacle Choir. She studied voice for years and auditioned several times, but she never made it, and she was really depressed. In the course of working with her, I found out that she had grown up on the wrong side of the tracks in Salt Lake City. She always thought that if she could get into this choir, she could prove that she was as good as other people. Once she had unlocked her *true* feelings, she realized that what she'd always wanted was recognition. After that it was easy to find a way to help her get it. Now she's happy and successful."

Happy and successful? But on whose terms? Certainly not according to her original desire. What this success coach had done was help this woman want what she could get, because he couldn't help her get what she wanted.

Now please don't misunderstand me. There is nothing wrong with being satisfied, happy, and contented with the material circumstances of your life. In fact, it is a blessing that far too few of us enjoy. Personally, I would be thrilled to see a book along the lines of *How to Want What You Have, When You Can't Have What You Want.* But success books and success coaches do not teach contentment; they teach the kind of material success that is recognized, pursued, and applauded by the secular culture, a culture that has little use for the message of service, submission, and sacrifice taught by Jesus Christ. Yet, like the success coach I encountered, self-help books fall far short of their goal, so they fill their pages with the inflated promises of "success" stories that defy logic and do not hold up to rational scrutiny.

In another flight of illogic, psychologist David Burns attempts to prove scientifically that self-help books are beneficial. He cites a study of sixty-seven depressed patients, half of whom were given self-help books to read. After four weeks, 66 percent of the book group had improved or recovered from depression while only 19 percent of the other group had.[6] As a trained scientist, I can only wonder that a scholarly journal would have accepted what would not even stand up to the scrutiny of a Master's thesis examining committee.

First, sixty-seven is a woefully inadequate sample size.

Second, the study tells us nothing about the types of depression involved, about double-blind randomization, or statistical analyses. Third, Burns tells us nothing about a control group—the research subjects who are given other kinds of books to read, say mysteries or romance novels or spy thrillers or science-fiction adventure stories. Finally, Burns gives no indication that the study was ever replicated. If the study is properly designed and the results are valid, an independent research group should be able to reproduce the experiment and get the same results. If not, the work and the researchers' conclusions are flawed.

The lay public needs to be very careful any time anyone claims scientific proof for anything. Just because a position sounds rational does not mean that it is. (Of course, the title of Burns's book, *Ten Days to Self-Esteem*, should give the reader some idea of the leaps of illogic that the author expects him to make.)

Withdrawal from reality

A *Newsweek* article tells the story of a Manhattan secretary who used to read the newspaper on the way to work. Now she reads positive affirmation books because she found the news too negative and depressing.[7] Once you have decided to abandon the intellect, it becomes easy to withdraw from reality.

Not only does the self-help movement tacitly promote a withdrawal from reality, but many self-help books actively encourage it. They warn readers against anything that will make them feel negative or threaten their self-esteem or raise uncomfortable questions about the self. In the world of self-help, *I* am the most important person, my ideas the most engaging, my problems the most critical. Reality simply does not enter into the self-help equation. Commenting on this abandonment of reality, historian Richard Hofstadter has written that self-help materials present a kind of belief in magic.[8]

Consider the category of self-help known as affirmation books. These little volumes contain daily sayings that are supposed to help people make their lives more positive. Affirmation writer and proponent Ruth Fishel defines an affirmation as more than a positive thought. It is something wonderful that we imagine and express about ourselves as if it were actually and immediately true. Furthermore, Fishel believes that if we repeat and experience our positive thoughts with utter conviction, they will become as true as we imagine them to be.[9] But can I really secure myself a spot on the U.S. Olympic equestrian team by daily telling myself that I am doing so? I suspect that Ms. Fishel fully realizes the limitations of her affirmations, because those that she uses to illustrate her points are so general, so subjective, that their effectiveness is almost guaranteed. If I tell myself, "I am allowing good things to happen to me today," then even getting a good parking space at the grocery store can be interpreted as "proof" that the affirmation works. A belief in the power of such statements is rather like a belief in the general horoscopes carried by most daily newspapers, and people who order their lives by such beliefs are simply out of touch with reality.

Trivialization of real problems

Homecoming author John Bradshaw insists that 96 percent of Americans come from dysfunctional families. Bradshaw is not alone in making such an amazing estimate. Self-help writers, judging from their books, consider most Americans as dysfunctional, identifying almost every behavior as "toxic" to some degree. Recovery programs exist for people who work too much, shop too much, exercise too much, sleep too much, eat too much or too little, watch television too much, read too many romance novels . . . The list is endless. And should you disagree with this assessment, you are dismissed as a person "in denial," which is another whole category of dysfunction.

Judging from the sales of self-help books, Americans agree with the writers' assessment of their problems. Certainly television talk shows bear witness to our proliferation of pain. Most of us have seen or at least heard about the endless parade of abused, victimized, or recovering people who air their past or present dysfunction for millions of voyeuristic viewers to clack their tongues over. It is true, sadly, that some people in our society suffer from the effects of terrible physical and mental abuse. They may come from homes where they are brutalized; they may seek escape in drugs or engage in self-destructive behaviors. But to insist, as Bradshaw and other self-help writers do, that the vast majority of Americans are dysfunctional is to trivialize the real problems of suffering people who need genuine help, not simplistic, one-size-fits-all answers. Writer Michael Brennan, himself a recovered drug addict, notes that the insistence of self-help experts that we are all victims devalues those cases where people suffer genuine abuse, genuine discrimination, genuine repression, genuine persecution.[10]

Lack of engagement with real problems

If the self-help movement trivializes personal tragedy by insisting that we are all victims of one sort or another, it completely refuses to acknowledge the real suffering of much of the world today. Each and every day countless millions of our fellow human beings face starvation, the atrocities of war, grinding poverty, and devastating diseases. In China women face forced abortions and involuntary sterilizations. Female babies are suffocated, their spines are broken, or they are simply left to die of exposure. In countries such as Ruanda and Bosnia, people have lived in fear for their lives, simply because of their ethnic background. There is real and terrible suffering in the world that makes the "pain" of a "shopaholic" not only laughable, but insulting to the rest of humanity.

Could it be that we people of privilege are so out of touch with real misery that we must create pseudo-problems for ourselves? Even a problem that would seem serious, such as nuclear proliferation, is a problem only for the rich. When you live in abject squalor, wondering how you will feed your children from day to day, or when you face the real and present danger of dodging a sniper's bullets simply to procure water for your family, nuclear destruction is not a big issue. Only those who have something to lose fear global annihilation.

Self-help addresses the "problems" only of privilege and wealth—addiction to food or work or sex, lack of self-esteem, personal success, happiness, and fulfillment. I cannot help wondering how self-help's strategies and tactics, its advice and programs, would stand up to the real problems of most of the world's population. Could positive visualization help a woman in the slums of Brazil feed her babies? How about positive self-talk or goal-setting? And how would this poor woman react to being told that "she didn't plan to fail, she just failed to plan"?

Focus on personal experience

One of the more striking features of all self-help materials is their heavy reliance on subjective reports, perhaps because they lack objective content or perhaps because personal experience is so hard to discount. Whatever the reason, self-help materials are replete with such anecdotes—case histories of dysfunctional people whose lives have been turned around by a recovery program, almost mythical tales of people who have achieved life-long goals by practicing a success writer's formula for fulfillment.

Subjective accounts serve both to inspire the reader to try a self-help program and to prove the program's efficacy. This personal experience, many self-help authors claim, is necessary before the reader can really understand and appreciate the program presented. The reader is never encouraged to consider the author's ideas on an intellectual level. Critical discussion, analysis, and logical evaluation are abandoned in favor of personal action. The inability of a particular reader to experience a program personally only points to his unwillingness to enter into the work of the program. It never indicates a failure of the author to present his material in an intellectually compelling and logically satisfying way.

This focus on personal experience, writes Robert Wuthnow in a statement that echoes Protagoras's dictum that man is the measure of all things, "makes the individual the measure of all things."[11] Gone is any carefully crafted creed, consensus, or inquiry. All that matters is how I feel about an issue or situation or system. The lessons of the past and the wisdom of scientists, philosophers, theologians, and sages throughout human history are less important than my opinion and my personal experience.

An emphasis on success and successful people

Because self-help materials rely so heavily on the evidence of personal anecdotes to prove their message, those anecdotes must, of necessity, illustrate success. The people held up as examples in self-help books may start out emotionally crippled or lacking self-esteem or victimized or unhappy or unfulfilled or impoverished in some way. But by following a self-help program, they become winners. The few examples of failures that self-help writers occasionally provide illustrate what happens to people who don't follow the course properly or, more often, deny the need for such a program.

Even ostensibly Christian self-help/inspirational books, such as Ben Carson's *Think Big*, are no exception. An African-American who rose from poverty to become a successful surgeon, Carson may write that we should never compare ourselves to others and may even maintain that a garbage collector is no better or worse than a lawyer, but the successful people Carson holds up as examples for his readers are all high-achieving professionals.

Not only do self-help books focus on success, but they make it clear that success is measured in terms of material wealth, position, and power. Dr. Carson, for example, may tell us that attitude, not wealth or prestige, determines success. But his examples are all of highly placed people who earn a great deal of money, people such as the doctor who owns six clinics, the senior partner in a major law firm, the successful talk show host. Carson's one concession to unsuccessful (i.e., not wealthy) people is that we should be as nice to them as we are to people in power.[12]

Reliance on easy answers

In *I'm Dysfunctional, You're Dysfunctional,* Wendy Kaminer rightly observes that people who regularly read self-help books are looking for easy answers to life's problems and for guarantees that those answers will work.[13] The writers of these books know exactly what their readers want, and they are quick to provide what the public is willing to pay for.

The answers offered by self-help writers typically cover a broad range of problems or needs and often involve a great deal of magical thinking. Barbara Sher, in one of her recent self-help offerings, tells readers that the secret to having whatever you want is simply knowing what that is.[14] Peter McWilliams and John-Roger explain that we can have anything by getting out of what is popularly known as our comfort zones.[15] And self-help multimillionaire Charles Givens repeats advice given by countless success consultants when he tells readers to compile a list of goals and keep it handy for daily reference.[16]

Other pearls of wisdom offered by self-help writers include practicing positive self-talk, keeping a journal of our true feelings, making a list of one's best attributes and achievements, using a six-most-important-things-to-do list, meditating, and even stretching. Norman Vincent Peale said we should practice picturizing, while the less homespun Napoleon Hill recommended positive visualization. Ben Carson says we need to think big.

The advice and answers of these self-help writers sounds simple because it is. Too simple. After all, merely visualizing myself as a success cannot and does not make me one. I may have physical limitations that block my goals. I may lack talent, intelligence, and resources. The truth is, life is never as simple as these writers would lead us to believe. For many people, success is a matter of sheer luck. For other people, it is the result of very hard work. And for still others, hard work proves fruitless. There are no easy answers because life is not easy. It is not even fair.

The sacrifice of truth to practicality

America is a results-oriented society. We expect to see results from our businesses, our medical system, our schools, and even our religions. Self-help literature is no exception, according to Richard Hofstadter, who has observed that what it offers is practical in nature.[17] Religious self-help writer Norman Vincent Peale, for example, did not write about the truth of Christianity, but about its usefulness, its pragmatism: "Christianity is entirely practical. It is astounding how defeated persons can be changed into victorious individuals when they actually utilize their religious faith as a workable instrument."[18]

This need for practical results cuts like a gash through the self-help that masquerades as American Christianity. According to Robert Wuthnow, who has studied small self-help groups extensively, we no longer judge our beliefs, our spirituality according to absolute standards of truth or goodness. Our spirituality is true only if it smooths our path through life. "If it helps me find a vacant parking spot, I know my spirituality is on the right track. If it leads me into the wilderness, calling me to face dangers I would rather not deal with at all, then it is a form of spirituality I am unlikely to choose," Wuthnow writes.[19]

The self-help movement, like American society at large, emphasizes this pragmatism. Positive affirmations don't have to be true; they only have to help me feel more positive about my life. Self-esteem programs are valuable if they make me feel better about myself, not if they reveal the truth about myself. I embrace what produces results. What does not work I discard. Truth is never considered.

The injection of a spiritual element

Self-help writers clearly recognize that human beings have a spiritual dimension that needs to be satisfied, regardless of our conscious, material view of reality. So it's not surprising that success books often talk about fulfillment and service and balance, not just bottom lines; self-esteem books about loving oneself as a key to loving God and others; recovery and affirmation literature about releasing the god within us. While this spirituality may be only a mush of pop psychology, New Age religion, and Buddhism, it is a far cry from the nineteenth-century obsession with emerging technology that left our great-grandparents feeling like cogs in a cosmic machine.

The Esalen Institute, famous for spawning the human potential movement in the 1960s, now talks about the midlife crisis as a spiritual emergence. Affirmation writer Ruth Fishel calls recovery a spiritual path. And Stephen Arterburn, co-author of *Toxic Faith,* claims that today's Alcoholics Anonymous meeting is closer to the community and behavior that Christ expects of us.[20]

Not even the self-help offered by exercise programs is free of this spurious spirituality. The hottest trend in health clubs is exercise combined with meditation/spiritual consciousness-raising. Programs at Crunch Fitness in Manhattan are labeled noncompetitive and nonjudgmental and are deemed ideal for recovering exercise addicts.[21] One devotee of the program has even called it church. Participants of such programs greet each other, make positive affirmations, and meditate around special candles before exercising, all to a fuzzy background of incense and New Age music. This is truly church for the unchurched, church for the 1990s overclass that has rejected the religion of its parents, but recognizes the need for religion nonetheless.

God/man role reversal

In the world of self-help, God becomes man's enabler, man's advocate, man's glorifier. Man, on the other hand, becomes the center of his spiritual life. God exists as an aide to that spirituality rather than as man's creator, judge, and redeemer. This view of God arises from self-help's pragmatism as much as from its spirituality. God can be useful. In books on self-esteem, we see God validating man so that he can love himself. In success literature, we see God rewarding man's efforts. In recovery, we see God leading the way back to health.

Richard Hofstadter notes that "what the inspirational writers mean when they say you can accomplish whatever you wish by taking thought is that you can will your goals and mobilize God to help you release fabulous energies."[22] Writing in the same vein, Robert Wuthnow asserts that small self-help groups are redefining spirituality, changing our understanding of God so that the sacred becomes more useful for fulfilling our individual needs.[23] And in *The New Republic*, writer Hanna Rosin notes that in the new seeker churches, where you can find everything from beauty classes to aerobics groups to anger workshops, Jesus has become the most effective antidepressant.[24]

A litany of platitudes

I have yet to read a self-help book in any category that does not rely heavily on platitudes—cutesy, fulsome sayings that are silly at best, insulting to the intellect for the most part, and dangerously misleading at worst. These platitudes say very little and mask the lack of real substance in most self-help material, rather in the way sound bites mask the lack of substance in political speeches. Here are a few common self-help sayings. I'm sure you've heard these and many others just like them many times.

> "Today is the first day of the rest of your life."
> "If you can think it, you can do it."
> "Winners never quit, and quitters never win."
> "You don't plan to fail, you fail to plan."
> "Never say never."

"God don't make no junk."

"There are no such things as problems—only opportunities disguised."

"Everyone is special in his/her own way."

"You have to believe it before you can see it."

"Eliminate the Do gap."

"Now is the only time you have."

An unremitting selfishness

Seeking self-gratification, self-fulfillment, and personal pleasure was once considered hedonistic or just plain selfish. But to the self-help movement, this behavior, now called "selfing," is good and healthy. Better than that, it is valid. People who practice selfing experience wholeness and the joy of nurturing their inner child.

Standing in opposition to selfing, we find behaviors once described as unselfish, selfless, and sacrificing. At one time in our history, these behaviors were considered virtues and were encouraged for the good of society. But according to self-help thinking, people who exhibit these traits are in denial; they refuse to express their true needs and wishes. Such denial can cause physical problems and interfere with healthy relationships, self-help writers tell us.

Typical of this attitude is *Spontaneous Healing*, one of the latest in the perennially popular self-help genre that I call self-healing books. Replete with anecdotes but no real science, this book includes, among many similar accounts of self-healing, the story of a man who apparently cured himself of back pain by ridding himself of his wife. One wonders about the pain his wife had to endure. Apparently, it wasn't considered worth noting. Also conspicuous by its absence was any mention of the man's marriage vows to his wife or his obligations to anyone other than himself. The salient point was that this man was able to free himself of his physical ailments by practicing the healthy trait of selfing.[25] I can't help hoping that someday someone will tell him that hell is the place where we have nothing left but the self.

2

How Did the Self-Help
Movement Begin?

When I first started researching the self-help movement in America, I was working under what is probably a fairly common assumption. I thought that secular self-help started around the time of Napoleon Hill's still popular *Think and Grow Rich* and that religious self-help had its origins in Norman Vincent Peale's *A Guide to Confident Living*. What I found was that self-help in America is much older and that it cannot easily be separated into different secular and religious movements. The two overlap in ways that make all self-help both secular and religious in nature, in the same way that the secular philosophies and theological schools of any given period in history tend to overlap, contributing to and influencing each other.

What follows are the movements that I believe to be influential in creating the modern self-help phenomenon. Each of these movements had its own version of self-help, the echoes of which can still be seen in one or more of today's types of the broader genre. It is not my intention to criticize any of these movements or to analyze them in any depth—only to provide a brief historical overview of self-help. The key word here is *brief*. For more in-depth information on these movements, I have included several good books in the Suggested Reading list.

My selection of various movements does not mean that these are the only trends in thinking occurring at various times in American history. America has always been a great melting pot, a society pluralistic in its ideas as well as its people. At any given period of history, many ideas were circulating, each with its own proponents, its own influences, its own consequences.

I did not, for example, choose to consider Hegelianism (which explains reality by suggesting that new "truths" are created from the synthesis of opposite views), even though it had profound effects on later thought. Nor did I include twentieth-century irrationalism (with its emphasis on feelings and instincts), which certainly contributed to some of the sillier ideas of self-help. What I tried to focus on were major movements that led to the development of American self-help.

I also recognize that many of these movements overlapped; their edges blurred into one another both philosophically and temporally. Some coexisted in time and occurred in tension with each other. Certainly, one movement did not end cleanly and another take its place. Puritanism did not end with the Enlightenment or with romanticism; its influence can be felt, and many of its ideas are current today. Not everyone in any given period agreed with the new ideas. We know that not everyone in our century is a logical positivist, believing that statements are true only if they can be conclusively verified by observation and experiment. So in the nineteenth century, not everyone was a pantheistic romanticist, although the influence of those groups could be felt throughout the culture.

What I hope will become apparent is that self-help is not just a modern phenomenon, although some forms of it, such as self-esteem teaching, have come into their own only in the last two or three decades. Nor is self-help the product simply of a selfish, self-serving, or hedonistic culture, although these features of modern American life have certainly allowed self-help thinking to flourish beyond anything that has occurred in other times and other cultures. Self-help seems, in some measure, to be a natural consequence of how Americans view reality and themselves. It is part and parcel of the American mythology that has lionized the rugged individual and the self-made man, that is suspicious of authority, and that believes wholeheartedly in personal success, happiness, and fulfillment.

Indeed, one could easily make a case that people willing to pull up stakes, break ties with their ancestral past, and build new lives on foreign soil are precisely the type of people who believe in the possibility of personal progress. That belief has shaped America, and it is not in itself wicked. Many of the movements that fostered self-help thinking in America, such as programs to educate disabled people and the crusade for universal suffrage, also contributed immeasurably to the public good. It is only when self-help becomes an exaggerated focus, when it is both the means and the end, that we begin to see the hand of Satan distorting a God-given virtue into an evil that is at best heresy, at worst idolatry.

PURITANISM

The influence of Puritanism on American thinking was so powerful because the Puritans' theology found expression in their daily lives and in the culture and politics of their time. Puritanism was not confined to Sunday services. It was carried into all aspects of secular existence. Indeed, for a Puritan, there could be no such thing as a purely secular part of life. Their theology gave the Puritans a way to both explain and control their world, to interpret and shape existence.

Professor Larzer Ziff, who has written one of the most comprehensive books on Puritanism that I have read, described the emergence of Puritanism in England as a way for common people in the sixteenth century to cope with masterlessness and land-lessness and all the hazards these conditions entailed.

The peasants found themselves without masters and without land because the rigid system that bound them to the property-owning lords was coming apart. This system was called seignorialism (or manorialism in England). The lords had controlled the lives of their serfs, even saying whom they could or could not marry. In return the peasants were given the right to hold (although not own) for their entire lives the land on which they made their living. That right was passed on to their heirs and could not be revoked.

In other words, if you were a peasant, the lord of the manor might be able to keep you tied to your work on his land, but he couldn't just throw you off the land if he took a dislike to you or found a harder-working tenant. You had no upward mobility, but at least you were assured of a job, a place to live, and food. You knew who you were, where you belonged, and what was expected of you. When this system broke down, the peasants were freed from the power of the lords, but they were also freed from the security of their inherited position on the land. According to Ziff, the Puritan way of life helped the newly freed peasant deal with his insecurity and make something of himself.[1] This is self-help at its most basic.

The single most important element of Puritan theology was the doctrine of election. So important was this doctrine that it affected every aspect of the Puritan's life, and its effects can still be seen today in the self-help movement. Briefly, election means that God chooses some people for salvation and some for damnation. When a person is chosen, or "elected," to receive God's grace, that person is touched by the Holy Spirit in a way that is irresistible. Conversion can be instantaneous, as the Apostle Paul's, or gradual. In either case, conversion is experienced in a personal way.

As a result of becoming a "gracious believer," several things, apart from eternal salvation, occur. First, the gracious believer, by possessing a conscience enlightened by conversion, becomes his own authority. According to Ziff, Puritans absolutely denied the chain of authority in the church. In its place, they enthroned the individual's conscience. The Puritan believed that the possession of an enlightened conscience allowed a man to become his own master.[2]

Second, by virtue of his election, the gracious believer is free to use all the things of this world because they are sanctified to him merely by virtue of his election. Thus, the Puritan was free to pursue commerce or any other worldly activity. More than that, this belief allowed the Puritan to look on nature as an ally, not an evil enemy of the righteous.[3]

Third, because all worldly pursuits become sanctified by association with the elect, the Puritan believed that it was his pious duty to perform all his works with diligence. Hard work was a mark of service to God, and hence a proof of election. One Puritan minister wrote about this service to a parishioner: "You honor God as much, nay, more, by the meanest servile worldly act, than if you should have spent all that time in meditation, prayer, or any other spiritual employment, to which you had no call at that time."[4] If God calls you to do business, then do it as well as you can. Being a good businessman is more important than prayer if business is your calling.

Finally, to prove you have been elected to receive God's grace, it is important that you succeed. How else can you demonstrate God's favor? In this sense, Puritanism aligned itself with pragmatism. The truth of their beliefs lay in the usefulness of those beliefs, the ability of those beliefs to enhance and improve their daily lives, to ensure their success. As is the case for self-help devotees today, Puritans looked on truth as an exercise in the practical.[5] But unlike today's thinking, Puritan beliefs also encompassed a sense of absolute truth that transcended the practical. An unsuccessful Puritan would not simply abandon his beliefs as untrue but would examine his life to see why God had withdrawn His favor.

The self-help ethic that emerged from Puritanism is easily

recognizable today. It includes an emphasis on personal experience, a belief in success through personal effort, the view of God as enabler and rewarder, and a heavy dose of pragmatism.

During the eighteenth century, this Puritan (i.e., self-help) ethic was popularized most notably by Benjamin Franklin who, although he rejected much of Puritan religious belief, remained Puritan in his thought patterns and practices. Through his writings, Franklin gave advice on acquiring wisdom, wealth, and happiness—still the popular topics of self-help literature today. And echoes of Franklin's banal maxims ("Early to bed and early to rise make a man healthy, wealthy, and wise." "A penny saved is a penny earned." "Time is money." "God helps those that help themselves.") can still be heard in the platitudes of today's self-help books.

Even in his personal life, Franklin embraced self-help. In 1727 he organized a few of his friends into what is unquestionably a small support group. Named the Junto Club, the group of twelve men (the number can hardly be coincidental) met every Friday night for, in Franklin's own words, "mutual improvement."[6] Franklin developed a set of "standing queries" that each club member was to read regularly. The queries clearly demonstrate Franklin's interest in both material and personal improvement and presage the common advice of today's self-help experts that we write down our goals and review them daily.

THE AGE OF ENLIGHTENMENT

While Franklin was a product of his Puritan background, he was also a man of the Enlightenment. He loved science and reason and apparently possessed boundless belief in the moral perfectibility of human beings. Enlightenment thinkers, such as Franklin, did not agree with the Puritans that personal moral authority, self-improvement, and success were the special preserve of God's chosen few. These benefits were available to all people through the exercise of human effort and, most important to the enlightened mind, through human reason.

Enlightenment thinkers also disagreed with the Puritans over the nature of God. While the Puritan God was personal, choosing and discarding humans at will, rewarding, punishing, always concerning Himself intimately with human affairs, the God of the Enlightenment was an impersonal deity who had created the universe, set it in motion, and then more or less washed his hands of the whole affair. From then on, everything, including one's destiny, was left to oneself. If you understood the laws that governed the universe, you could exploit those laws for your own advantage. This concept bears a striking similarity to the assertion of modern self-help books that success is simply a matter of understanding and following certain success laws or formulas or programs.

While the Enlightenment had several effects on Christian theology, the two most important for our discussion of self-help are:

1. The emphasis on the inherent goodness of human beings, their freedom, and their importance in their own salvation—the Arminian rather than the Calvinist view of humanity.

2. A belief in physical and moral progress, carried out by a person's own efforts, that would eventually lead to a practical kingdom of heaven here on earth.

You can see the influence of these beliefs in the writings of theologians such as Daniel Whitby and Samuel Clarke, men who disagreed with the doctrines of limited atonement, predestination, even the Trinity, and whose works led the way to Universalism.

The self-help movement as it exists today rests firmly on the beliefs of the Enlightenment. After all, what is the point of pursuing success, happiness, self-esteem, or personal fulfillment unless you first believe that all persons have within themselves the ability to achieve these ends?

REVIVALISM

The First and Second Great Awakenings represented more than renewals of religious piety in America. Their goal to spread the Gospel throughout America and abroad ushered in a new era of reforming zeal marked not only by revival meetings and mission-ary programs, but also by humanitarian reforms and the rise of utopian socialism.

While the purpose might have been to spread the Gospel, the revivalist focus on publishing and Christian education (which led to the formation of the American Bible Society in 1816, the American Education Society in 1826, and the American Sunday School Union in 1824) helped make education and books of all sorts universally available. Education for the handicapped also began during this period, led by men such as Dr. Mason F. Cogswell of Hartford, whose daughter was deaf and dumb, and the Reverend Thomas Gallaudet. Reformers also tackled condi-tions in prisons and insane asylums.

This type of reforming, evangelistic zeal appears in much of self-help today. The typical success seminar, for example, bears a striking resemblance to a religious revival meeting. "Converts" to success or self-esteem or happiness or recovery programs often establish new groups to spread the word and educate the public.

Of particular note in the revivalist era was the rise of small groups—Sunday schools, missionary alliances, temperance clubs—voluntary organizations of people who banded together to accomplish a common goal. In 1797, for example, a group of Yale students formed a Moral Society. Before long such groups sprang up throughout the state and then throughout the nation.[7] In addi-tion to these small groups, the reforming spirit of the revivalist era led to the formation of large communities or societies, such as the Oneida Community founded by John Humphrey Noyes. The formation of groups and societies, both to accomplish shared goals and to encourage community members, is a standard feature of today's self-help movement. Modern recovery, support, and accountability groups all hearken back to revivalist societies.

Finally, the reformers of America's revivalistic period saw America as the second Eden, a God-given opportunity for man to put things right, to create a literal heaven on earth. The American citizen was a new Adam, and human progress was inevitable. This view of America as more than just a land of opportunity, but a divinely blessed country remains with us today in the work of many Christian self-help writers.

ROMANTICISM

The romantic era was marked by emotionalism, idealism, and spiritual mysticism. It spawned mystical religious movements, such as Swedenborgianism, and quasi-religious movements, such as transcendentalism. The romantic thinkers valued personal experience above reason as tools for explaining and comprehending reality. In the Christianity of this period we see a theology exemplified by the work of Friedrich Schleiermacher, who denied the value of traditional apologetics and established Christianity as a religion that could be understood only through personal experience.[8] The romantic did not try to explain or prove but to experience. This was the age of sensibility, not sense.

Chief among the American romantic writers and philosophers was Ralph Waldo Emerson. He influenced not only the American, but also the European thinking of his day. Emerson advocated self-reliance and may have been the first writer to tell Americans to do their own thing.[9] In his now-famous (or infamous) address of 1838 to the graduating class of Harvard Divinity School, Emerson presented a theology that is more pantheistic than Christian. He argued that the creative mind "is everywhere active, in each ray of the star, in each wavelet of the pool" and that "all things proceed out of the same spirit."[10] And in his essay "In Tune with the Infinite," Emerson states clearly, "In essence the life of God and the life of man are identically the same, and so are one."[11] Similar statements about the nature of man and God are being made today in many self-help writings, particularly self-esteem, affirmation, and inspirational works.

In that same address, Emerson stressed the paramount importance of personal experience in terms that anticipate today's relativistic insistence that values are personal. "What he announces, I must find true in me, or reject; and on his word . . . be he who he may, I can accept nothing."[12] Here again, we see that external authority is rejected for personal, internal experience. The scholarly work, the years of study, the careful investigation of a learned professional are not as important as the individual's feeling on any subject.

Like many of today's self-help/inspirational writers, Emerson wrote and lectured about love, friendship, and selfhood. He was instrumental in forming the Transcendental Club in 1836, a group that included other important romantic thinkers, reformers, educators, and writers—luminaries such as Henry David Thoreau, Margaret Fuller, Theodore Parker, and Bronson Alcott. These transcendentalists advocated self-examination and individualism, insisted that God could be found in everyone and everything, and glorified human beings. In this way transcendentalists are probably closer to modern self-help than any other past school of American thought.

The success writers of Emerson's day enlarged on his theme of self-reliance and flooded the American market with endless tales of the self-made man. How-to-be-successful handbooks and manuals flourished as never before. Cities, towns, and villages, however small or distant, were inundated with books offering prosperity-generating principles, according to Louis B. Wright, who studied the phenomenon.[13] Given the enormous proliferation of success books today, it appears that very little has changed.

The mood of the romantic thinkers had definite effects on Christian inspirational writers of the day who, although not embracing anything like Emerson's pantheism, still stressed personal experience and the importance of the inner life. An example of this trend is Charlotte M. Yonge's *Gold Dust.* Published in 1880, Yonge's book advocates the "hidden contemplative life of the soul."[14]

THE AGE OF ANALYSIS

Once again the pendulum sways, and twentieth-century thinking swings away from the romantic and toward the logical, the analytical. Popular trends in thinking during our century include materialism, realism, pragmatism, instrumentalism, and existentialism. Any philosopher reading this is probably cringing at my cavalier lumping together of these different schools of thought. Nevertheless, and realizing that what I am about to suggest is an oversimplification, I will rush in like the proverbial fool and make the observation that while they may differ in their major focus, all of these "isms" share some important features.

They all reject the notion of an absolute, they agree that matter exists apart from any human perception of it, they view knowledge as something that can be verified by personal experience, and they insist that truth is relative to circumstance. In addition, these schools of thinking are concerned largely with man's physical existence. In some cases, as in materialism, physical existence is the only existence; man and the universe exist as a result of purely natural, not supernatural, phenomena.

These beliefs are crucial for modern self-help. A belief that matter is what really counts not only gives us permission to pursue material wealth and worldly success, but it makes such a pursuit the only logical way to spend one's life, because nothing beyond or outside of this life exists. A belief in pragmatism allows me to define truth in my own terms and lets me focus on the pursuit of my own values, because they are the only values with meaning for me. I, the individual, the self, am the measure of all things.

Religious writers of the twentieth century have reflected this material view of existence. Christian Science, for example, emphasized earthly peace, comfort, and success. Material affluence was a demonstration of religious truth.[15] And writers such as Orison Swett Marden, Norman Vincent Peale, and Robert Schuller have churned out a large body of books and periodicals about winning, success, and using religion for material gain.

Perhaps the most important offspring of the analytic age, at least for the development of the self-help movement, is psychology. Today the various schools of psychology dominate our thinking about the nature of man, the origin and development of consciousness and personality, human bonds, altruism, selfishness, virtue, crime, passion, reserve, self-esteem, success, failure. Psychology has endeavored to explain almost every aspect of human existence. In fact, without the overwhelming influence of and fascination with psychology, the self-help movement would probably not be as far-reaching as it is today. Why? Because psychology gives us permission to be preoccupied with ourselves. While other philosophies may deal with the nature of truth or meaning or knowledge, psychology is interested only in the human organism—how it thinks the way it does, why it behaves the way it does. By insisting on the importance of the self and self-knowledge, psychology provides the ultimate justification for making truth subjective and personal experience paramount.

THE NEW AGE

A preoccupation with material existence left modern man spiritually empty. He couldn't quite bring himself to believe in a personal God or a life after death. Science and reason had delivered the kibosh to those ideas. Nevertheless, he yearned for something outside himself to give his life meaning. And so dawned the New Age. So popular is this movement that New Age beliefs on wellness and wholism have become almost cliche.

The New Age movement sparked a new interest in Eastern mystical religions, with their focus on inner reflection, meditation, and self-knowledge, and their promotion of what a popular cartoon movie has called the circle of life. Man is a thread in a cosmic fabric of existence, no more or less important than all the animate and inanimate objects that also make up that fabric. Gone is the need for an Absolute to which we are answerable and which sets the standards for our conduct.

Zen Buddhism is one of the fastest growing religions to express the New Age sentiments in America. It is well suited as a religion for a secular age because it has "no God to worship, no ceremonial rites to observe, no future abode to which the dead are destined. Zen has no soul . . . whose immortality is a matter of intense concern."[16] Buddhism fills modern man's need for a spiritual center without making any serious demands. Truth remains relative. Man remains the focus of his existence.

Increasingly, modern self-help reflects the New Age philosophies. Even material success writers talk almost as much about balance and wholeness as about goal-setting and prioritizing. Many health clubs operate as if they were Zen temples. Recovery programs and self-esteem workshops include strategies on meditation.

From the age of the Puritan to the New Age, self-help has been a fixture in American culture. It may shift its focus, gain ascendence, or lose ground, depending on the tone of the time, but it never quite disappears, because it represents a historic longing in Americans to have more, to do more, to understand themselves more, to be more. That longing can produce crass and shameful results, as in the "name-it-and-claim-it" gospel. Or it can save lives, as in Alcoholics Anonymous.

The problem is that while self-help programs may begin with worthy motives and goals, they often degenerate into self-serving agendas. The Puritans, for example, originally believed that business is a way of serving God. But over time, the distinction between divine service and service to self disappeared. Religion became just another business tool, a way of using God for worldly success.[17]

As human beings, our motives are never pure, our actions always flawed. To believe that self-help is the way to personal success, whatever the goal, is to deny human nature. That self-help persists and, in fact, is gaining ground in our culture as a spiritual answer is an indictment of Christians. We have failed to communicate the Gospel in a way that transforms individual lives and society.

3

What Sustains the Self-Help Movement?

Crazes, fads, rages, novelties. Call them what you will, those ideas that capture the popular imagination are usually a flash-in-the-pan affair; here today and gone tomorrow; now you see them, now you don't. So how do you explain the self-help movement's phenomenal staying power? Yes, its popularity may have risen and fallen many times during America's 200-some-odd years. But it has never completely disappeared. And how do you account for the almost unprecedented interest in self-help since the 1960s? The answer, I believe, is multifaceted and ranges from the purely practical to the mythological.

MONEY

There's no getting around it. The self-help movement is big business. There's money to be made, and a lot of it, through books, audio and video tape programs, seminars, and lectures. It is estimated that twelve million Americans participate in about 500,000 self-help groups.[1]

In an article aptly titled "Possessed!" free-lance writer Steve Salerno notes that Americans, particularly women, buy millions of self-help books every year.[2] According to *Publisher's Weekly*, the megasellers of the 1980s were self-help books promoting material success and physical perfection.[3] While the 1990s seem to be less me-oriented than the 1980s, self-help books continue to dominate book sales. An analysis of *Publisher's Weekly* best-seller lists reveals that upwards of two million self-help/inspirational books were sold in 1991, including books about assisted suicide, financial success, and personal achievement.[4] And nearly half of *PW*'s 1994 list of longest running hardcover bestsellers, books such as *Embraced by the Light* and *Stop the Insanity*, fall into the self-help/inspirational categories. *PW*'s 1994 list of longest running paperback bestsellers also include a liberal supply of such books, including *The Road Less Traveled* and *7 Habits of Highly Effective People*.[5]

In a recent television interview, the authors of the self-help/inspirational book *Chicken Soup for the Soul* estimated that they would each make several million dollars next year from the sales of that book alone. So successful is the book that plans are underway to publish sequels targeted for specific subgroups in our population.[6] According to the authors, *Chicken Soup* sells love, hope, and self-esteem. It seems that the American appetite for books of this sort remains insatiable.

Religious publishing has not escaped from the effects of the self-help craze. According to *Christianity Today*, recovery books are big business in Christian publishing, even in evangelical houses. Thomas Nelson, for example, has published and is enjoying tremendous sales of a New Testament that includes essays for people in twelve-step recovery programs.[7] And *Chicken Soup for the Soul* authors are working on a sequel for Christians, something like *Chicken Soup for the Christian Soul*. This venture of Christianity into the self-help market has many critics worrying that the gospel message is being distorted as God is sold in the American marketplace.[8]

With so much money to be made, it behooves marketing experts, advertising professionals, and sales forces to keep the pot boiling, to generate as much interest and excitement in these products as possible. Infomercials, talk shows, and personal appearances by self-help experts are designed to convince people that they need these books or tapes or seminars to make themselves happy and successful and fulfilled. Television "teasers" show clips from success meetings that would be the envy of Billy Sunday. Participants cheer for themselves and their seminar leaders; they shout slogans; they raise their hands in song. Throw in a few shouts of "washed in the blood" and "praise Jesus," and you'd have an old-fashioned tent revival. Emotion sells, as any professional salesperson will tell you.

ANTI-INTELLECTUALISM

People who stop and evaluate a message, who apply the rules of logic and reason, who engage their intellect in the practice of daily living are not particularly good candidates for the self-help business. Because modern self-help rests firmly on a set of lies (which we will consider in the next section), it promotes anti-intellectualism to maintain its market and prevent discovery. After all, for self-help advertising to work, it must convince people to buy something they don't need by describing it in ways that cannot possibly be true.

This was not always the case. America's original self-help movement, that of the Puritans, was anything but intellectually impoverished. The Puritans believed in truth and in the integration of faith with daily life.[9] Their concern for the development of the mind can perhaps best be seen in their involvement in establishing Harvard University, still the standard for excellence in scholarship. And Benjamin Franklin, who popularized secular self-help in the eighteenth century, was a man of letters and a champion of education.

Not so today. When education is encouraged by pop culture, it is to get a better job or make more money, not to enrich the mind, not to develop a citizenry that can evaluate ideas critically, not to contribute to an aesthetic that sees beyond MTV rock videos and Clio award commercials. The self-help movement today, with its insistence that we are all either in recovery or denial, that we are all victims of some sort of abuse, that we can all be successful, that we should all pursue our heart's desires, is part of and contributes to what journalist Carl Bernstein has called "the weird and the stupid and the coarse" in today's idiot culture.[10]

The self-help movement today may be simple-minded. But by using the tools of advertising and the power of mass media, it has been wildly successful at convincing people that hedonism is acceptable, that what they want is the same as what they should have, and that self-actualization, not self-sacrifice, is the true bedrock of civilization. And all the while self-help engages in this campaign of deception, no one bothers to ask whether it is really rational to believe that anyone can become rich by writing down and reciting his goals daily. The fact is, if it were that simple, we would all be wealthy, happy, successful, whole, and fulfilled.

THE AMERICAN MYTH

America is the land of opportunity. Why else would millions of immigrants have endured unimaginable hardship to get here? They believed, indeed the whole world may still believe, that in America (and perhaps only in America) going from rags to riches is truly possible. The country bumpkin, through dint of hard work, moral fortitude, and single-mindedness, rises from his roots in a log cabin on the American frontier to become a wealthy philanthropist, chief executive officer of a major banking house, or president of the United States. Look at Abraham Lincoln, James A. Garfield, John Jacob Astor, and Cornelius Vanderbilt. What more proof do you need?

The myth of the self-made man or woman is as popular today as it was in 1832 when Henry Clay coined the phrase. He said that "almost every manufactory known to me is in the hands of enterprising self-made men, who have whatever wealth they possess by patient and diligent labor."[11] Today's self-made men and women are just as lionized as those of Henry Clay's time. Today we have our Tony Robbins and Charles Givens and Steven Covey, men who have not only risen to the top and made enormous fortunes, but who have realized that self-help offers them an even broader avenue to wealth than simple "manufactory." These men know that you can make money by doing something, but you can make a fortune by convincing other people to do it. These men have so much power today, and their message is so accepted without question, that they are regularly consulted by our political leaders. These public officials set the agenda of our country in ways that are far more important than the colors of next year's automobiles.

Clearly, Americans believe in the myth of the self-made man, in the beautiful dream of personal advancement, success, fulfillment, and happiness, despite an impoverished start in life. But how does this American myth measure up to the reality? Not very well, according to Irvin G. Wyllie:

> Sociologists, business historians, and others have piled up mountains of impressive statistical data to prove conclusively that a majority of our wealthy citizens do not now, and never did, come up from the ranks of the poor. Through all our history the self-made man was the exception not the rule. American opportunities have been magnificent, but they have never equaled the aspirations of the whole people; success has been for the few, not the many.[12]

MAGICAL THINKING IN AN ADOLESCENT CULTURE

By historical standards, the United States is something of an adolescent. So to understand certain features of our culture, it may be helpful to look at the characteristics of adolescence. Just remember, this comparison between a culture and a person is useful as an analogy only. After all, a culture is not a person, adolescent or otherwise; it is a society's lifestyle—a sum of the artistic, intellectual, and behavioral expression of a society's people.

Adolescents have tremendous strengths and weaknesses, which can also be seen in the character of American society. Adolescents are energetic, fun-loving, sociable, and fearless. They are also somewhat paranoid, self-involved, insensitive of others, and undisciplined. They aren't really sure of who they are, and so they regularly try on different personalities, different clothes, different hairstyles. They want to be free and independent, but they are afraid of responsibility. They are often excessively emotional and sometimes unpredictable.

America is a vigorous nation, enthusiastic and inventive. We take up and drop new ideas with reckless abandon. We lead the world in innovation. The Japanese may be great developers of technology, but that technology has its conception and birth in America. We are friendly and outgoing, yet rude and vulgar. We insist on the freedoms of our democracy and the noninterference of the federal bureaucracy, yet we expect the government to bail out our failing cities or businesses, support us in our old age, protect our environment, and keep criminals at bay.

Adolescents and American society share another common feature. We are both guilty of magical thinking. In adolescents, magical thinking typically takes the form of a belief in immortality. Although intellectually they know better, most adolescents act on the subconscious belief that they cannot die. The adolescent cannot envision his own demise, much less his susceptibility to accident or disease. Perhaps that is why accidents are the leading cause of death for teenagers. They are careless in the magic of their power. They don't wear seat belts in cars or helmets on motorcycles; they drink and drive; they engage in dangerous sexual practices.

In American society, magical thinking takes several forms, including a belief in our boundless superiority and limitless opportunities—the American myth. The mythology of America, the rags-to-riches story, works because our magical thinking has convinced us that it is true. Evidence such as that presented by Wyllie doesn't phase us. Similar statistics on the failure of American education, on the widening gap between rich and poor, on growing levels of unhappiness and dissatisfaction in America don't affect us. We are America, and everything wonderful can happen here, even the attainment of unimaginable wealth and personal satisfaction. We only need to know the secret, and self-help experts are more than willing to provide that. Self-help succeeds because we want to believe in its magic.

THE GRAIN OF TRUTH

Despite all the hype, all the misrepresentation, all the snake oil, even all the silliness, and despite our almost incomprehensible gullibility, modern self-help would not exist today were it not for the tiny grain of truth in it. The truth is that there are, indeed, ordinary people who have made a fortune in real estate speculation, people who have found healing in twelve-step programs, people who have improved their lives through self-esteem programs, people who seem to heal themselves of physical ailments through a positive attitude or imaging or laughter. After all, Wyllie's statistics show that the self-made individual in America is an improbability, not an impossibility.

This week's lottery ticket probably won't hit the jackpot, but it might. The latest self-help book probably won't turn my life around, but who knows? Just as poor Americans who can least afford to buy lottery tickets continue to purchase them in the hope of striking it rich, so emotionally and intellectually impoverished Americans keep buying self-help books, hoping that the next one will have the magic formula that will make them happy or successful or fulfilled.

Why is a grain of truth so powerful? The answer has a lot to do with the way biological organisms work. When I was an undergraduate, my major field of study was sensory and perceptual psychology—how we process sensory input and why we perceive the world the way we do. One of my courses covered the history of psychology. In it I learned probably more than I will ever need to know about behavioral conditioning. I learned that the fastest and easiest way to keep an animal performing a certain task is to reward it on a variable schedule. The animal knows only that it will be rewarded eventually if it keeps performing the task. But it never knows precisely when the reward will appear. So the animal keeps at its task endlessly, working for the occasional and unpredictable reward. (This is the type of reinforcement that keeps compulsive gamblers feeding quarters into slot machines.) A variable schedule is far more effective than, say, a fixed schedule in which the animal quickly learns that after five (or ten or fifteen or whatever the number) repetitions of its task, it will be rewarded. Should the researcher or animal trainer forget to deliver the reward at the expected time once or twice, the animal will quit working.

I think the grain of truth in self-help operates like a variable schedule paradigm. We don't know when the reward will appear for practicing our daily affirmations or positive self-talk or goal-setting or twelve-step programs, but we're certain it will. We have all heard enough success stories to know that the reward is real, that it will happen. We just don't know when. So we keep buying the books or tapes and attending the seminars or lectures or small groups.

But the most devastating aspect of self-help's grain of truth is not that it keeps us coming back for more, but that it serves as an excellent launching pad for Satan's attacks. It is, after all, far easier to convince someone of a distorted truth than an outright lie. And there are truths in self-help, quite apart from their on-again, off-again success rate. People do need a certain amount of self-esteem. Some people do suffer from real addictions and can be helped by twelve-step programs. We are in some measure responsible for and capable of effecting our own happiness and fulfillment.

But what we have to remember is that Satan takes these rather minor truths and distorts them, making them all important in our lives. He tells us that our self-esteem and self-love and self-fulfillment and success and happiness are our birthright and our first responsibility, the goals we must seek before we can be of use to others or to God. It is through such distortions that he takes our eyes off Christ and turns our focus inward and, in so doing, erects a barrier between us and God. Too late, we find ourselves alone with the self that we have so carefully crafted. What is this place where the self exists in isolation? It is the abode known as hell.

So when we get right down to it, we see that the real sustaining power behind the self-help movement is the power of Satan himself. As Christians, we need to recognize that "our struggle is not against flesh and blood, but against the rulers, against the authorities, against the powers of this dark world and against the spiritual forces of evil in the heavenly realms."[13] Our enemy is not the foolish shopaholic or the exercise guru or the New Age crystalist or the success seminar junkie. They are victims of Satan's self-help campaign. And if his self-help wins in capturing the minds, the imaginations, and the souls of more and more Americans, it is because we Christians have failed to offer them what they really need—the Gospel of Jesus Christ.

PART II

The Lies of the Self-Help Movement

4

Lie One:
I Belong to Myself

In C. S. Lewis's *The Screwtape Letters*, senior devil Screwtape
writes to his nephew, the junior tempter Wormwood:

> The sense of ownership in general is always to be encour-
> aged. The humans are always putting up claims to own-
> ership which sound equally funny in Heaven and in Hell
> and we must keep them doing so. Much of the modern
> resistance to chastity comes from men's belief that they
> 'own' their bodies—those vast and perilous estates, pul-
> sating with the energy that made the worlds, in which
> they find themselves without their consent and from
> which they are ejected at the pleasure of Another! It is as
> if a royal child whom his father has placed, for love's sake,
> in titular command of some great province, under the real
> role of wise counsellors, should come to fancy he really
> owns the cities, the forests, and the corn, in the same way
> as he owns the bricks on the nursery floor.
> We produce this sense of ownership not only by pride
> but by confusion. We teach them not to notice the differ-
> ent senses of the possessive pronoun—the finely graded
> differences that run from 'my boots' through 'my dog,'

'my servant,' 'my wife,' 'my father,' 'my master' and 'my country,' to 'my God.' They can be taught to reduce all these senses to that of 'my boots,' the 'my' of ownership. And all the time the joke is that the word *mine* in its fully possessive sense cannot be uttered by a human being about anything.[1]

Ownership is a major issue for human beings and, if you agree with Lewis, as I do, a fairly obvious and simple point of attack for Satan and his lies. Because we use our possessions to define ourselves and to give ourselves a sense, albeit irrational, of control and security in what modern man perceives as a chaotic world, ownership can become a driving force in our lives. Jesus clearly understood the importance of ownership for human beings when He warned His followers not to lay up treasure on earth: "For where your treasure is, there your heart will be also."[2]

Just studying the word *ownership* will tell you why human beings attach so much importance to it. The *Oxford English Dictionary* defines ownership as right of possession, involving property, proprietorship, and dominion. The word *ownership* carries connotations of supremacy, authority, and power. Both common and statutory law recognize these attributes of ownership. If I own something, I alone am entitled to say what is done with it, as long as I don't break any laws or interfere with another person's rights. I can, for example, destroy my own house, but I can't destroy my neighbor's house (a felony), and I can't try to collect on the insurance policy (fraud). (Of course, I can't destroy my house by blowing it up, because the use of explosives is strictly controlled in my town. I can, however, invite the local volunteer fire department to burn down my house as a training exercise.)

Ownership has a biological basis, and God has given a sense of ownership to animals to help ensure their survival. Ownership among animals usually involves territory, because territory is necessary for both individual and species survival. Without a defined and defended territory, many animals would die of starvation. And in several animal species, the male must possess a territory in order to attract a mate and reproduce.

Ownership among humans is obviously more complicated, more abstract, but it shares a feature with animal territoriality. That feature is power. For an animal, that power is the ability to survive and maintain its place in the gene pool. For a man, that power is the ability to control. I control what I own. The more I own, the more control I have, and the more powerful I am. Furthermore, my possessions allow me to control other people. My power grows. In American culture in particular, to possess much is to be powerful. To possess little, to be poor, is to be powerless.

Human ownership, however, differs from animal territoriality in a significant way. We not only own objects, our means of power, but we claim ownership to something animals don't even recognize—the self. (What teenager—or, for that matter, what adult—has not shouted, "It's my life!" when faced with unpleasant and external demands?)

Where did we get the idea that we own ourselves? On what basis do we claim self-ownership? How do we become owners of anything? Human beings recognize ownership through creation, purchase, and gift. We own what we make, what we buy, and what we are given.

Creation probably provides the greatest claim to ownership. A novelist, for example, always owns the product of his creation. You may buy his book or even many copies of his book, but all you will ever own are pages and ink. The words will always belong to the author. Similarly, you don't really own a picture of your children taken by a photographer. The photographer owns the picture. You only own particular pieces of paper—the prints you have purchased. (If you don't believe me, check with a local photography studio. You may be surprised to learn that it is illegal to make a copy of your child's picture.)

Purchase is the most common means of ownership. We all buy things, usually exchanging money or goods or services for the things we need or want. But sometimes the desired object can be purchased only through drastic action, such as civil disobedience or even war, and paid for with loss of freedom, social ostracism, persecution, even death. Suffragettes bought the vote; black civil rights activists bought their place in the front of the bus; the United States bought its sovereignty; Baptists bought their religious freedom—all with a far greater price than a 20 percent down payment and a fifteen-year note at 9.8 percent interest.

The third basis of ownership—ownership by virtue of gift—is probably the least satisfying, because it usually necessitates some gratitude on our part. (In fact, the larger the gift and the more gratitude that we feel called upon to express, the more uncomfortable we become around the giver.) Nevertheless, it is by virtue of gift that we humans claim ownership over ourselves.

Life, the common reasoning goes, is given to us by nature or by our parents or by God. (Who the giver is depends on one's philosophic or religious viewpoint.) What we do with that life is then our choice and our responsibility. There is an element of truth in this belief. If there were not, Satan would not be able to use it so easily for his own purposes. What is that truth? That our lives are a gift and that we are free to use them as we wish. What is the lie? That the gift confers ownership.

We do not in fact own ourselves. What we have been given is the *use* of ourselves, rather in the way that the heir of an old family estate inherits its use for his lifetime. He holds the estate in trust for the next generation. And while he can farm the land, rent out the cottages, and use the proceeds of the estate in any way he pleases, while he can improve the estate or allow it to run to rack and ruin, he cannot sell or give the estate away, because he does not own it. Nor do we own ourselves. We merely hold ourselves in trust for God.

Once we truly understand that we do not own ourselves, the "self" loses importance. The self is not *our* treasure but God's. That being the case, we have no valid reason to place our hearts—

our attention—on the treasure that is ourselves. I have no reason to value the self that is me any more than I value the self that is you. When we die to our own particular self, all selves become valuable, and we are, for the first time, able to carry out the great command to love others as we love ourselves.

Self-help puts us in direct opposition to Jesus' teaching. The goal of self-help is to make us more aware of ourselves, not less. To be successful—to keep people buying books and tapes, attending seminars, joining support groups, and seeking "professional" guidance—the self-help movement must convince people that it is not only normal to place themselves first in their thoughts and actions, but that it is "healthy" to do so. Psychologist Abraham H. Maslow is a typical proponent of that mistaken belief. According to Maslow, people who are self-actualizing and self-fulfilled are mature and healthy. He sees them as almost a new breed of mankind and lauds them for exploring man's ultimate possibilities—for pushing the envelope, if you will.[3]

Self-help books commonly tell readers that women who put themselves first make better mothers and wives; men who pursue their own deepest needs are happier and more successful in all areas of their lives. Most of these books (and I have read scores of them) present the same list of assumptions.

We all have gifts.

We are all wonderful and unique.

We all deserve happiness and love.

We all need to get in touch with our true feelings.

We all need to visualize ourselves as successful.

We all lack a true appreciation of ourselves.

We all need to learn to love ourselves before we can love others.

We all need to put ourselves and our needs first if we are to be of service to others.

This relentless focus on the self would not be possible if it were not assumed first and foremost that we own ourselves, that we alone have the right to determine what is done with our lives and time.

Some self-help books make a more obvious statement of self-ownership than others. Pop psychologist Wayne Dyer makes no bones about this belief when he urges patients to be their own person and to resist anyone who tries to interfere. Dyer recommends his book *Pulling Your Own Strings* for people who want freedom more than anything else, who want their lives to be unrestrained.[4] In a similar vein, Leo Buscaglia tells his readers that personhood is their inalienable right; it is not a gift, as some would suppose.[5]

Best-selling author Terry Cole-Whittaker makes it clear that we should not accept any outside claims to ownership over our lives. She decries any notion that we need to be accepted into heaven and rescued from hell, the latter a place she claims to have been in and survived.[6] Apparently, not only does Cole-Whittaker own herself, but she can determine her own eternal destiny without so much as a passing nod to any outside authority. To bolster her claim of self-ownership, Cole-Whittaker tells readers that they can become their own creators, free of any constraints that would arise from the ownership claims of Another. And she recommends her book to women who want to know and reaffirm themselves without any constraints from external cultural, religious, or moral standards based on fear. Women, she believes, can create both themselves and their own world.[7] Remember, creation is the highest claim to ownership.

Other self-help books are more subtle, tucking the self-ownership message within almost incomprehensible jargon. A recent popular self-help book accomplishes this goal by inventing the new word *selfing*. Using this word allows the authors to encourage selfishness and a belief in self-ownership without resorting to words with negative connotations. "Selfing," they write, "means doing for one's Self [the authors' capitalization], in the larger sense of Self, as in True Self, or 'To thine own self be true.' It means fulfilling the dreams, goals and aspirations inherent within us. Selfing is putting yourself first in the abundance of now."[8]

Reading this, I can't help seeing C. S. Lewis's Screwtape whispering diabolical nothings in the authors' ears. And I can't help wondering if the authors ever studied *Hamlet*. "To thine own self be true" is part of Palonius's speech to his son Laertes. Palonius's advice, as any Shakespeare scholar will tell you, was a mass of self-serving platitudes. Today we might say, "You have to look out for Number One."

Ostensibly Christian self-help writers also rely on the lie of self-ownership. Echoing Maslow's belief in health and selfhood, Lewis B. Smedes, Professor of Integrative Studies at Fuller Theological Seminary, insists that self-ownership is a sure sign of health.[9] Smedes also tells us that we own our raw materials and encourages us to take pride and joy in the self we own.

CONSEQUENCES OF THE LIE

The lie of self-ownership has serious consequences for our lives, for the lives of those around us, and for society. While I am not suggesting that the self-help movement has caused certain problems in the world, I am saying that it contributes to these evils by encouraging a belief in this lie of self-ownership.

Idolatry

The first and most obvious consequence of the lie of self-ownership is idolatry. By putting ourselves at the center of our thoughts and wills and existences, we usurp the place that God intends only for Himself. More than that, by claiming to own ourselves, we claim an attribute that only God can possess. That attribute is autonomy.

An autonomous being exists independently of any outside force. It is self-determining, self-sufficient, and completely free.

"What is autonomous freedom?" asks Francis Schaeffer in *Escape from Reason.* "It means a freedom in which the individual is the center of the universe."[10] But only God can be at the center of the universe. By claiming that humans are autonomous, the self-help movement encourages people to become their own god.

Like Schaeffer, Sigmund Freud understood the implications of autonomy. Unlike Schaeffer, he believed that man should strive for this godless freedom. Political scientist Jeffrey B. Abramson claims that Freud developed a therapy in which the patient gains freedom by learning how to be a "virtuoso" of the self.[11] Even a cursory look at the self-help movement shows that its goal is to make each of us a virtuoso of the self—perfect in our individuality, answerable to no one but ourselves.

Some self-help/inspirational writers don't waste time on preliminaries such as human freedom and autonomy, but tell us straight out that we can be gods. One such author, Barry A. Ellsworth, asserts that not only is God love, but I am love also.[12] It doesn't take an advanced course in logic to understand that if A is B and C is B, then A is C. In other words, I am God.

In another inspirational/self-help book, two Canadian authors, Ian Kent and William Nicholls, have committed what I consider blasphemy when they write about two "authentic selves" coming to know each other. When those two selves are merged, the result is, they proudly proclaim, I AM THAT I AM.[13] Kent and Nicholls have gone one better than Satan, who only promised Eve that she would be *like* God. They have promised us that we will *be* God. How? By discovering the self.

Not to leave women out of this god business, Terry Cole-Whittaker encourages her female readers to get in touch with the goddess within. The experience, she says, is just what our tired, old planet needs. When we awaken our powerful and loving goddess, the earth will come of age.[14]

In his major bestseller *The Road Less Traveled,* M. Scott Peck attempts to turn the idolatry of the self-help movement into a spiritual quest sanctioned by God:

What is it that God wants of us? It is not my intention here to become involved in theological niceties, and I hope the scholarly will forgive me if I cut through all the ifs, ands, and buts of proper speculative theology. For no matter how much we may like to pussyfoot around it, all of us who postulate a loving God and really think about it eventually come to the single terrifying idea: God wants us to become Himself (or Herself or Itself). We are grow-ing toward godhood.[15]

Peck is right about one thing. His idea is terrifying, and anyone who is entertaining it would be well advised to prostrate himself before the living God and beg forgiveness! (Actually, he's also right about his disregard of what he calls theological niceties. But then heresy has always flourished in an atmosphere of ignorance.) What is also terrifying to me is that Peck's book can be found in most Christian bookstores and often finds its way into adult Christian education curricula. There's even a study guide to help groups explore the book in depth!

Relativism

Along with the belief in autonomy that arises from the lie of self-ownership is a belief in relativism. Since I own myself, since I act as an autonomous being, and, as we have seen, since I am god, I alone have the authority to decide what is true for me. My expe-rience, my knowledge, my view of reality, my personal circum-stances are all different from yours. You can no more decide what is true for me than you can decide what clothes I will wear or what food I will eat on any given day.

Relativism is responsible for much of what evangelical Christians see as moral decay in our culture. The argument com-monly given in support of abortion, suicide rights, and homosex-uality, for example, results from the relativism made possible by the lie of self-ownership. Since I own my body and my life, I alone decide what is moral for me and how I will use my body. No one has the right to force me to carry an unwanted fetus in my body. No one can prevent me from voluntarily ending my life, and no one has the right to condemn my sexual practices.

This relativism can be seen in the self-help books of both secular and Christian writers. Secular author and therapist Irene C. Kassorla notes that winners are aware that life is short, so they pursue goals that give their lives meaning according to self-determined values and standards.[16] In a similar vein, Jesuit Leo P. Rock insists that the most important thing for us are our own thoughts on any subject. He admits that we can learn from the thoughts and experiences of others. But he maintains that others' thoughts are valuable only when they shed light on our own experiences.[17] Apparently, nothing has any objective meaning or value apart from my experience.

Another Christian self-help writer, Dale Hanson Bourke, who advises women on how to fulfill themselves, has included a chapter on values clarification in her book *You Can Make Your Dreams Come True*.[18] While Christian writers such as Bourke may not be advocating abortion or homosexuality, by encouraging readers to look within themselves for their values, they unwittingly foster the environment that denies absolute truth or an outside authority that sets our standards and governs our behavior.

Secular humanism

The goal of the self-help movement is a sort of new and improved person. The implication is that individuals, on their own, are capable of perfecting themselves. (Apparently, just being god is not enough. We have to be the best god that we can possibly be.) In their book *Born to Win*, psychologists Muriel James and Dorothy Jongeward state that everyone is born with the wherewithal to win and that everyone can be a winner through his or her own efforts.[19] And in *Psycho-Cybernetics 2000,* a rehash of Maxwell Maltz's quasi-religious behavioral system, psychologist Bobbe Sommer promises that by following the book's simple, practical program, the reader can empower himself to do all kinds of wonderful things, such as create the ideal job, reduce stress, increase earning potential, achieve a happier and healthier love life, and build a success-achieving personality.[20]

Religious writers, like their secular counterparts, see human beings as capable of helping themselves. Leo P. Rock, S. J. says that we need to explore our relationship with ourselves first and then our relationship with God and other people.[21] By exploring that relationship, Rock says, we can achieve great things.

Man owns himself, he judges his own values, and he can perfect himself with his own efforts. This belief is nothing short of secular humanism. Humanism, writes Christian apologist Josh McDowell, is the belief that every day in every way, we are getting better and better.[22] Secular humanism asserts that "man's goal is the development of his own personality" and that "man will continue to develop to the point where he will look within himself and to the natural world for the solution to all of his problems."[23] The Humanist Manifesto II expressed the common position of modern self-help literature in its assertion: "While there is much we do not know, humans are responsible for what we are or will become. No deity will save us; we must save ourselves."[24]

Aggression

The animal behaviorist looks at human aggression and sees a connection between man and his animal ancestors. Man the aggressor is merely man the animal acting on orders from his primitive brain systems that help him survive in the natural world of predator and prey. The theologian looks at human aggression and sees fallen man in active rebellion against God.

The foundational lie of the self-help movement, the lie of self-ownership, encourages man's rebellion. In *Who Speaks for God?* Chuck Colson warns that "the search for fulfillment through self-discovery has always been doomed from the beginning." One reason, Colson explains, is that "a by-product of searching for meaning within the four walls of self is this—the search inevitably excludes the community of which we are a part."[25]

The self-help movement leaves us with fallen man, full of himself, excluding all others. This exclusion commonly takes the form of aggression. Twentieth-century theologian Reinhold Niebuhr also warned us about this man: "The ego which falsely makes itself the center of existence in its pride and will-to-power inevitably subordinates other life to its will and thus does injustice to other life."[26] And as if that weren't frightening enough, Niebuhr goes on to quote Pascal: "This I is hateful. . . . In one word it has two qualities: It is essentially unjust in that it makes self the center of everything and it is troublesome to others in that it seeks to make them subservient; for each I is the enemy and would be the tyrant of all others."[27]

WHAT THE BIBLE SAYS ABOUT HUMAN OWNERSHIP

From Genesis through Revelation, a recurring theme in Scripture is that human beings belong to God. This concept is most eloquently expressed in Psalm 100, perhaps one of the best known of all the Psalms. "Know that the LORD is God. It is he who made us, and we are his; we are his people, the sheep of his pasture."[28]

Human beings base their tenuous claim to self-ownership on the rule of gift. How does God lay claim to us?

First, God claims human ownership through the act of creation. "Through him all things were made; without him nothing was made that has been made."[29] While we may use our bodies and the world around us, like the reader who uses a book but does not own its words, we do not own ourselves. The Author does.

Second, God claims the right of human ownership through purchase. As the Apostle Paul explained to the Corinthians, "Do you not know that your body is a temple of the Holy Spirit, who is in you, whom you have received from God? You are not your own; you were bought at a price. Therefore honor God with your body."[30] The price that God paid for human beings was the blood of Jesus, His own blood. Again Paul reminds the Ephesians, "In him we have redemption through his blood, the forgiveness of sins, in accordance with the riches of God's grace that he lavished on us with all wisdom and understanding."[31] What is redemption? The act of buying back.

Finally, God owns us through the right of gift. All creation was made by the Father, through the Son and for the Son. All of creation—and that includes you and me—was intended as a gift of love from God the Father to God in the person of Jesus. "He is the image of the invisible God, the firstborn over all creation. For by him all things were created: things in heaven and on earth, visible and invisible, whether thrones or powers or rulers or authorities; all things were created by him and for him."[32]

In a vision, Daniel saw this gift hundreds of years before God shattered human history with the Incarnation. "I kept looking in the night visions, and behold, with the clouds of heaven One like a Son of Man was coming, and He came up to the Ancient of Days and was presented before Him. And to Him was given dominion, glory, and a kingdom, that all peoples, nations, and men of every language might serve Him."[33] Isaiah also predicted God's gift of love to Jesus. "In love a throne will be established; in faithfulness a man will sit on it—one from the house of David—one who in judging seeks justice and speeds the cause of righteousness."[34] And John's Revelation told of the gift: "The kingdom of the world has become the kingdom of our Lord and of his Christ, and he will reign for ever and ever."[35]

Clearly, we belong to God—lock, stock, and barrel. As Christians, we need to give more than mere lip service to this fundamental truth. Unfortunately, many Christian self-help books try to convince us that we have an obligation and a freedom to focus on ourselves because God expects us to develop the talents He has given us. (Jesus' parable of the talents is generally offered as proof.) What these books fail to consider is that God may not intend to use our talents in working out His plan for creation. In

Who Speaks for God? Chuck Colson quotes from an article he admits to reading with sadness. According to that article, "God gives us freedom to be whatever we like. He gives each of us a unique, authentic self and then encourages us to discover it, nurture it and expose it to others." Colson's response? "God does indeed create us with distinct individuality and gifts. But nowhere have I been able to find the premise in Scripture that He has left us to define what constitutes our personal authenticity. Rather, I find that God has a sovereign plan for our lives which we discover, not in seeking ourselves, but in seeking His will."[36]

Despite what all the Christian self-help and inspirational books may say, the simple fact is that God comes to us in our sinfulness and works through our failures and weaknesses for His greater glory, because His "power is made perfect in weakness."[37] Chuck Colson is a perfect example. God did not use Colson in his power and privilege, when he had the ear of a president and Washington at his feet. God used Colson in his disgrace. We could all accomplish great things if we had at our disposal an army of high-achieving, well-educated, articulate, beautiful, healthy, powerful men and women. Only God could transform the world with peasants and criminals. God does not need our talents. He wants our lives which are, after all, His property.

5

Lie Two:
I Am Entitled to a Life
of Happiness and Fulfillment

I began working on this chapter with a fair degree of trepidation. After all, who in his right mind would malign happiness? Certainly not me. I have no doubt that it is better (or at least it feels better) to be happy than unhappy. Like self-esteem, happiness produces many desirable results, both for happy people and for those with whom they come in contact.

Social psychologist David G. Myers has recently analyzed the impressive body of research on happiness. He concluded that "happy people are strikingly energetic, decisive, flexible, creative, and sociable. Compared to unhappy people, they are more trusting, more loving, more responsive. Happy people tolerate more frustration. They are less likely to be abusive and are more lenient. Moreover, in experiment after experiment, happy people are more willing to help those in need."[1] Who could take exception to such an overwhelming litany of virtues?

True or not, most people seem to believe that happiness is the greatest good a person can aspire to. More than two thousand years ago, Aristotle wrote that people seek happiness more than anything else. Certainly Myers believes, and with some empirical evidence, that given a choice between happiness or our usual goals—money, power, fame, physical health, and beauty—most of us would choose happiness. Psychiatrist Harold H. Bloomfield believes that we pursue happiness as a natural consequence of our basic biological and psychological make-up.[2] And Dr. Alan Epstein, cofounder of True Partners, a marriage brokerage rather euphemistically called an introduction and relationship counseling service, says simply that most people want to be happy.[3]

So while I don't dispute that happiness can be beneficial or that most of us place a great deal of importance on it, I do take exception to the popular belief that happiness is a fitting goal for human beings. All of which brings me to what I believe is the second most important lie of the self-help movement, the lie that I am entitled to a life of happiness and fulfillment, that I can and should actively seek happiness, that happiness is my birthright. This lie figures prominently in the major recurring themes of happiness "how-to" books:

Everyone can be happy.
Everyone should be happy.
Happiness comes from understanding yourself.
Happiness comes from loving and accepting yourself.
Happiness comes through personal enlightenment.
Happiness comes through practicing happy thoughts.

When listed in this way, the themes of happiness books sound almost silly and trivial. But this is exactly what these books expect us to believe, starting with the mind-boggling notion (at least from a Christian perspective) that we are somehow born happy, that happiness is our natural state. Stress management consultant Dr. Richard Carlson teaches that joy is our natural state of mind.[4] But if that were truly the case, why does Carlson feel the need to add, on the very same page of his book, that few people ever achieve happiness? How can it be difficult to achieve something that is a natural state? In its natural state, diamond is very hard indeed. It does not need to achieve or work at the state of hardness.

Despite this logical inconsistency, Carlson is not alone in his belief that happiness is our natural condition. Maharishi Mahesh Yogi, who pioneered transcendental meditation in the United States, said that all we have to do is start enjoying our natural state, which is one of bliss.[5] TM trainer and devotee Dr. Bloomfield says that transcendental meditation allows us to get in touch with our natural happiness.[6] And according to Dr. Jane Nelson, our natural state of mind includes inherent good feelings.[7] Ken Keyes, Jr., who writes about personal success despite extreme physical hardship, has noted that people who aren't consistently happy are failing to take advantage of their natural state.[8]

Now I agree that some people seem to be born happy, if by happy you mean a cheerful disposition, a merry spirit, a tendency to look on the bright side of life. Anyone who has spent any amount of time with newborn babies knows how different their personality tendencies are, right from the start. Some babies cry a great deal for no apparent reason. Some are naturally quiet. Some watch everything around them. Some seem more inner-directed. Some newborns relax and cuddle into your arms when you pick them up. Others become rigid. Fortunate is the baby (and especially the parents of that baby) who has inherited a sunny disposition.

Incidentally, I use the word *fortunate* deliberately. The English word *happy* has as its root the word *hap*, which means luck or fortune. The hapless person, for example, is unlucky. The happy person is fortunate. The expression "happy is the man" that we find in so many Bible verses usually refers to a state of good fortune, not merriment or optimism or a sense of well-being and contentment—the ways we usually define happiness today.

(And, no, I am not advocating a belief in luck, nor am I saying that the Bible advocates such a belief. What I am saying is that sometimes things just happen to people, like their hair color or the shape of their nose or an ear for music or a good disposition. Some people may grow up in warm, loving homes; some people in nasty, spiteful ones, all through no fault or merit of their own. As a result, it may just be easier for some people to be nice or happy or outgoing or charitable. C. S. Lewis talks about this in *Mere Christianity* and tells us that this is one reason we should never judge another person.)

So some people are probably born with naturally sunny, optimistic, contented dispositions. But they are the blessed (or happy or fortunate) few. I don't think that even happiness writers who propose that happiness is mankind's natural state really believe their own assertion. Why else do their books focus on "secrets" or "formulas" for happiness? These formulas range from the just plain silly, telling us that we should put more joy into whatever we do by just doing it (sounds like an athletic shoe commercial, doesn't it?); to the practical, telling us we'll be happier if we get a good night's sleep; to the esoteric, telling us that we just need to find ourselves in order to be happier.[9, 10, 11] Alan Epstein has given us an entire year, day by day, of happiness exercises, including brief explanations of their effectiveness. Some of his happiness suggestions include getting dirty, doing something naked, and sending ourselves a happy postcard.[12] I don't know about you, but this advice sounds a trifle inane to me.

Both Bloomfield and Native American Billy Mills advocate meditation as the way to happiness. Calling it the secret of happiness, Mills even provides a meditation exercise to be performed three times a day that, he insists, will allow us to be happy all the time.[13] Working from a more scientific background, Bloomfield's TM advice includes lots of information on the limbic system and pleasure responses, implying that meditation stimulates the part of your body that makes you feel good. Apparently, for Bloomfield, human happiness is the same as animal pleasure. Psychologist Harold Greenwald has provided a seven-step happiness program that reads like most of the success plans in how-to-get-rich books, starting with a decision about what you need to make you happy and ending with the admonition that you support yourself in that decision.[14]

Even ostensibly scholarly works, such as Myers's recent book, wind up giving us the "secrets" of happy people. While Myers says he isn't advocating any particular behaviors to help people become happy, nevertheless, he gives us a very usable list of things that enable happiness. Commenting on this list, Myers himself says that while his book is really only meant to inform, it would be foolish not to take advantage of its information to become happier people.[15] In other words, do this and you'll be happy.

Almost without exception, happiness writers claim that happiness is an attitude and that the key to happiness is personal mind control. Happiness workbook author Nancy Ashley insists that we are what we think and that we can all create our own reality.[16] Richard Carlson says the key to happiness is the mind, and he tells us that we are only a single thought away from a good feeling.[17] Billy Mills tells us that happy thoughts will make us feel good.[18] Happy thoughts? Tinker Bell said happy thoughts could make you fly until a few gullible children tried and were injured. Hence the addition of fairy dust to the Peter Pan story.

Not to be left out, religious writers also peddle positive mental attitude. Robert Schuller tells us that we can find happiness in readjusted mental attitudes. To support his point, Schuller has co-opted the Beatitudes, calling them "be-happy attitudes," and telling us that they provide the spiritual motivation to become happier.[19]

Schuller is not the first or the only happiness writer to use Scripture as a happiness formula or to focus on the Beatitudes. John-Roger and Peter McWilliams talk about happy attitudes, renaming them, predictably, be-attitudes.[20] Billy Graham's *The Secret of Happiness,* written forty years ago and revised and reissued in 1985, also presents the Beatitudes as a formula for happiness.

While it may be true that the Greek word for "blessed," found in the Beatitudes, can also be translated as "happy," and while it may also be true that happiness, contentment, and joy may result from practicing the virtues of the Beatitudes, I think we are stretching a point to assume that Jesus was giving us His happiness secret. The Beatitudes deal with the ethics of God's kingdom. They are presented in a common Old Testament literary form, and, according to Craig S. Keener, professor of New Testament at Hood Theological

Seminary, "the blessings are the promises of the kingdom for those who live the repentant life. Jesus' hearers would have understood them especially as promises for the future time of God's reign."[21]

Furthermore, Jesus' ethical teachings were not meant for everyone. They were directed specifically to His disciples, people who had undergone the change necessary for them to understand and follow such hard lessons. Remember, God expects a very different standard of behavior from His people than he expects from the world. (Incidentally, if you're interested in a truly Christ-centered reading of the Sermon on the Mount, I recommend Dietrich Bonhoeffer's *The Cost of Discipleship*.)

Other religious self-help writers are just as sold as Schuller is on the notion that happiness is a fitting goal for people. Louis Schneider and Sanford M. Dornbusch, who analyzed forty-six best-selling religious inspirational books, observed that this literature concerns itself with happiness in the here and now. Furthermore, the happiness these books offer does not rely on resignation to the will of God. More than that, Schneider and Dornbusch found that these books tell readers to *expect* happiness in this life.[22] The happiness advocated by many of these religious writers is trivial and silly at best. At worst, it is insulting to people who struggle not only with real unhappiness in their lives but with real tragedy, real hardship, real danger—people who face starvation, war, or debilitating diseases.

Norman Vincent Peale, one of Christianity's most popular happiness advocates, advised people that they could choose to be happy or be miserable every day of their lives.[23] Peale insisted that anyone can do this, despite all of life's trials. By way of illustration, he recounted the story of a vacation trip to the mountains of West Virginia that could have been spoiled by snow. But by changing his attitude, he was able to stay happy and enjoy the vacation. Did Peale honestly believe that a snowy vacation was a trial that needed to be overcome by practicing a happy attitude? What of the countless millions of people who don't know what it is to have full bellies, much less vacations?

Still not convinced that happiness is touted as a fitting goal by self-help writers? Consider this. Happiness writer Richard Carlson says that happiness doesn't lead anywhere because it is the destination, the goal itself.[24] In *Looking Out for #*1, Robert J. Ringer tells readers that their main objective is happiness.[25] In *Over the Top* (which, incidentally, is published by the evangelical house of Thomas Nelson), Zig Ziglar says that we can make happiness a specific goal.[26] And on a recent television magazine show, Maria Shriver looked at the search for happiness by Americans, a search that has led many of them to quit their jobs, sell their houses, or cash in their retirement funds to attend eight-week classes at The Option Institute. Defined by the State of Massachusetts as a tax-exempt, nonprofit, religious, educational institute, this organization claims to teach happiness. Former advertising executive Barry Kaufmann runs it.[27]

What the happiness researchers and writers, be they scholarly or metaphysical or spiritual, have apparently not considered is the cause-effect problem. Do happy people exhibit certain behaviors or characteristics because they are happy, or do certain behaviors and characteristics make people happy? Myers, for example, seems to recommend altruistic behavior as a means of achieving happiness. But does altruism really make you happy? Or do happy people feel so good that they naturally reach out to others? This is not merely a problem of semantics. I am not splitting hairs. Answering this question is fundamental to our understanding of happiness.

As I see it, this question raises some of the same issues as does the Christian problem of grace and works. Paul, under the inspiration of the Holy Spirit, teaches us, "For by grace are ye saved through faith; and that not of yourselves: it is the gift of God: Not of works, lest any man should boast."[28] Nevertheless, works are a mark of grace; they flow naturally from our love for God, which is only possible because of the grace God has given us. We cannot become people of grace by doing good works.

In the same way, optimism, energy, charity, tolerance—all of Myers's observations about happy people—may well be the result, not the cause, of happiness. I may be optimistic or tolerant or helpful to others because I am happy. But optimism or tolerance itself may not make me happy. And in any event pursuing any activity for the purpose of personal gratification, as Myers and other happiness writers seem to suggest, gets us right back to the problem of putting the self at the center of our attention.

ORIGIN OF THE LIE

Where did we get this idea that we are entitled to happiness? In America we have written this right into our most sacred political document, the Declaration of Independence.

> We hold these truths to be self-evident, that all men are created equal, that they are endowed by their Creator with certain unalienable Rights, that among these are Life, Liberty, and the Pursuit of Happiness. That to secure these rights, Governments are instituted among Men, deriving their just powers from the consent of the governed. That whenever any Form of Government becomes destructive of these ends, it is the Right of the People to alter or abolish it, and to institute new Government, having its foundation on such principles and organizing its powers in such form, as to them shall seem most likely to effect their Safety and Happiness.

And with that revolutionary statement, the world received a new vision of government's origin, role, and responsibilities. Government does not exist at the pleasure and discretion of God, deriving its authority and power from God. Government exists by the will of mankind. Nor does government exist as God's instrument on earth to check man's naturally sinful and rebellious nature. Rather, government exists to secure for mankind those rights given to him by God and which cannot be taken away. Chief among those rights is Happiness, the only right to be mentioned twice in this most famous of paragraphs.

The founding fathers who crafted the Declaration of Independence reflected the thinking of the Enlightenment. They were fully convinced that man could and should pursue his own perfection, his own happiness, quite apart from any outside influence, be it king or god. God may exist, an afterlife may exist, but man's business is to improve his life in the here and now.

Enlightenment republicanism, with its mistrust of the governing abilities of the masses, soon gave way to democratic populism. Individuals were sovereign, and the common man was perfectly capable of participating in government. Now happiness could and should be pursued by everyone, with each person judging happiness for himself. As Os Guinness has observed, "the right to personal judgment became the Magna Carta of the Common Man."[29] Populism remains a dominant influence today and can readily be seen in our rejection of authority, our celebration of the "man-in-the-street" wisdom, and especially in our "do-your-own-thing" attitude. That attitude finds fullest expression in our relentless search for happiness.

A final and significant "happiness" influence should be mentioned here. And that is the entertainment industry. From television to movies to music videos to romance novels to trendy magazines, the message is the same. If it feels good, do it. If it makes you happy, go for it. You deserve the best. Americans are constantly being told they deserve to feel sexually fulfilled, they deserve to take exotic vacations, they deserve to drive luxury cars, they deserve to live in beautiful surroundings. And because they deserve all this happiness, they shouldn't have to work or wait for it. So they deserve a gold credit card.

CONSEQUENCES OF THE LIE

Dissatisfaction and disillusionment

The lie of happiness is crucial to the self-help movement. If you believe you are entitled to happiness, then just about anything you do in its pursuit is justified. If my relationship with my spouse makes me unhappy, I get rid of my spouse. If my church fails to meet my needs, I change churches. If my children cause me pain, I neglect them or, worse, abuse them. If you own something that will make me happy, I am entitled to take it, whether it is one of your possessions or even your body. The American obsession with happiness has led to a litany of personal and societal crimes, from broken relationships to frivolous litigation. Indeed, it is this belief that I deserve to have anything that I think will make me happy that has led to the recent rash of crimes against tourists in Florida. The children who committed these crimes explain them the same way we explain all of our behavior. I want what I want. Why should someone else have something I don't have?

But not even the happiness writers are so naive as to suppose that possessions can really make us happy. So in spite of all the advertising that encourages greed and conspicuous consumption, in spite of the overtly materialistic slant that marks all television programs, happiness writers tell us that true happiness lies within ourselves, not in what we own. But what these writers have failed to acknowledge, perhaps because the truth is too painful or too commercially fatal for their books, is that we are no more capable of making ourselves happy than are our possessions. So in the final analysis, any pursuit of happiness, by any strategy, is also doomed to failure. And we are left with the dissatisfaction and disillusionment so common to modern American life—we have seen it all, heard it all, done it all, and we aren't impressed.

Denial of pain

If we believe that happiness is our natural and fitting state, then what do we do about pain? In modern American culture, the accepted response to pain is to ignore or deny it, to medicate it away, or to surgically remove it. We are a society so committed to the pursuit of pleasure that we have no philosophy to help us account for or deal with pain.

And so when pain comes, as it inevitably does to all of us, we are surprised and affronted. Pain and suffering are vulgar; those who exhibit pain in front of us are guilty of the worst possible taste. We avoid those who are experiencing pain; we walk past the homeless without seeing them; we even malign those in pain, accusing them of causing their own suffering or, at best, refusing to heal themselves. The poor are guilty of their own poverty, the cancer victims of their own tumors.

This attitude is, in some measure, a holdover from the Puritan days in which right living was rewarded in obvious, materialistic, earthly ways. We don't want to believe, with Lewis, that pain is God's "megaphone to rouse a deaf world."[30] We refuse to believe that righteousness can be achieved only through the pain of poverty, grief, humility, hunger, and persecution. But then, who needs righteousness when you can have happiness?

Heresy

For Christians the most important and the most dangerous consequence of the lie of happiness is heresy. Carlson's assertion that happiness and contentment are our natural state borders on an ancient heresy called Pelagianism, which denied fundamental Christian teaching about the sinful nature and desperate condition of fallen mankind. This idea is not only foolish; it is damnably foolish. To believe that happiness is our natural state is to deny the Fall, to deny that the relationship between God and man is broken, to deny the need for redemption. If I am naturally a creature of contentment, and if I can create my own happiness through an exertion of my own will, why do I need Christ's sacrifice? I can save myself.

But God has planted within us a longing for the joy that C. S. Lewis calls "the serious business of heaven."[31] We do not long for that which is our natural state, but for that which we need in order to become the creatures God intended us to be. And so, rather than being naturally contented or happy, we are ever restless, searching, and uncomfortable. We may see glimpses of Joy, but not even the most devout Christian can live within Joy here on earth.

Furthermore, the lie of happiness, as interpreted by the religious writers who tell us that the Bible gives us the secret of happiness, leaves many people with the mistaken impression that worldly happiness is God's goal for us. This sort of God is "not so much a Father in Heaven as a grandfather in heaven—a senile benevolence who, as they say, 'liked to see young people enjoying themselves,' and whose plan for the universe was simply that it might truly be said at the end of each day, 'a good time was had by all,'" wrote C. S. Lewis.[32] Does God want us to be happy? Maybe. But first God wants us to be righteous, and He's determined to make us so, whether the experience is pleasant or not, whether it makes us happy or not.

Even worse, the lie that happiness should be our goal leads us away from God. Man does not find his happiness or contentment or joy or completion in God, but in other, often pagan, pursuits. Teilhard de Chardin writes that we achieve joy by uniting ourselves with the whole current of life. In this pantheistic expression, he links happiness with an impersonal, amorphous life force rather than with a righteous and personal God. And just in case you don't find the life force a sufficiently compelling reason for happiness, Chardin goes on to recommend that we sink our own interests and hopes in those of the world in order to be happy.[33]

Other happiness writers don't even bother with quasi-spiritual or altruistic feelings about the current of life or the greater good of mankind. They unashamedly espouse the rights of the individual to happiness on his own terms. Happiness advocate Jane Nelson, for example, tells us that when we are living in our natural happiness state, we should not be bound by rules, which only make us feel insecure.[34] Whether Nelson realizes it or not, she has provided a wonderful description of hell, where each individual pursues his own happiness without rules or boundaries or controls.

WHAT THE BIBLE SAYS ABOUT HAPPINESS

Far from being silent on the subject of happiness, the Bible tells us exactly how God views human happiness, pleasure, joy, and blessedness. And it tells us how we should approach happiness here on earth.

Happiness is expected of us.

"The settled happiness and security which we all desire, God withholds from us by the very nature of the world: but joy, pleasure, and merriment He has scattered broadcast. We are never safe, but we have plenty of fun and some ecstasy," wrote C. S. Lewis.[35] Fun? Merriment? Ecstasy? Absolutely. The Scriptures acknowledge what we all know from personal experience: life can be fun and exciting. It feels good to laugh, to cuddle a baby, to eat good food, to sing praises to God, to watch a sunset, to read a good book. Even washing the windows feels good (when you're finished and the sun comes sparkling in, making the outdoors look exceptionally beautiful).

The Bible makes it clear that we are to *enjoy* the world God has given us. We are to sing and dance and experience pleasure in praising God, in raising children, in sharing the company of family and friends, in eating and drinking. Zechariah tells us that holy festivals are a time for happiness.[36] In Genesis Leah expresses her happiness over the birth of Asher,[37] and in Psalms both mothers and fathers are expected to be happy about the gift of children.[38] In the New Testament, James tells us to sing songs of praise when we're happy,[39] and Paul comments that Titus is happy because his fellowship with the believers has refreshed his spirit.[40]

Happiness is a gift.

Throughout the Bible, we find that happiness is expected of us as people of God. But more than that, we find that happiness is not something we do for ourselves or find within ourselves or create by a positive attitude; it is something that we are blessed with, that God has given us. The ecclesiast tells us that "to the man who pleases him, God gives wisdom, knowledge and happiness."[41] To find satisfaction in your toil, he says, "This is the gift of God."[42] And again, "when God gives any man wealth and possessions, and enables him to enjoy them, to accept his lot and be happy in his work—this is a gift of God."[43] And the ecclesiast reminds us, "When times are good, be happy; but when times are bad, consider: God has made the one as well as the other."[44] God is sovereign, and everything we have, including our happiness, is His to give us, ours to gratefully accept.

Happiness is associated with righteousness.

Throughout the Bible, we see happiness (or blessedness, depending upon the translation) either juxtaposed with righteousness or resulting from righteous behavior. David sings a prayer that God's enemies may be scattered: "But may the righteous be glad and rejoice before God; may they be happy and joyful."[45] And in another song, David sings, "Blessed is every one that feareth the LORD; that walketh in his ways. For thou shalt eat the labor of thine hands: happy shalt thou be."[46] The ecclesiast tells us, "I know that there is nothing better for men than to be happy and do good while they live."[47] Doing good seems inexorably linked with being happy.

Happiness is associated with pain.

The Bible makes it clear that we should consider ourselves fortunate (or blessed or "happy") when we suffer, either from God's discipline as He works to perfect our righteousness or from the results of our discipleship. Job understood this lesson clearly: "Blessed (the King James version says "happy") is the man whom God corrects; so do not despise the discipline of the Almighty."[48] In the New Testament, Jesus taught His disciples that kingdom ethics, though they may entail the pain of poverty or grief or humility, have been ordained by God for our happiness. And Peter spoke of the pain we suffer as Christ's disciples, a pain that should be our joy, our glory, our happiness. "But if you should suffer for what is right, you are blessed" (or "happy" in the King James version).[49] "If you are insulted because of the name of Christ, you are blessed, ("happy" in King James) for the Spirit of glory and of God rests on you."[50]

When I read these words, I can't help wondering about the anger and invective pouring from "Christian" political groups, who are furious that their Christianity exposes them to the ridicule and intolerance of secular America. What did they expect? We have been told clearly that we will suffer for Christ's sake and that we should welcome such suffering with open arms. After all, if the world doesn't look askance at us Christians, then perhaps we are not living according to God's standards. The world should feel threatened by Christianity. Truth always threatens complacency, ignorance, and self-righteousness.

Happiness is not a goal.

I can find no passage in the Bible that even remotely implies that happiness is a fitting goal for mankind. Happiness may be desirable under certain circumstances, may be pleasant, certainly has its place, but it is not a goal. In fact, God even dictated a form of clothing the Israelites were to wear "that ye may look upon it, and remember all the commandments of the LORD, and do them; and that *ye seek not after your own heart.*"[51] This is the major difference between self-help logic and kingdom logic. Self-help tells us to pursue happiness. Jesus tells us to seek God's kingdom and His righteousness.[52] And if we are to find God, we must look for Him with all our heart and with all our soul.[53] Surely such an all-consuming pursuit can leave us little time to seek our own happiness or pleasure. But what inexpressible joy we will find when we find God.

6

Lie Three: I Was Born to Greatness

Royalty. Wealth. Greatness. These are man's natural state, his condition at birth, according to one self-help writer who believes that this is not only truth, but great truth.[1] This writer is not alone. Every self-help book I have ever come across expresses the same sentiment, either explicitly or implicitly. These books tell us that the ability to win, to achieve, to succeed, to conquer, to heal, to find ourselves, to become whole—to be great—lies within us. We are born this way. We just need to find it, uncover it, exploit it. We just need to believe in ourselves.

And the message never varies despite the individual background or personal expertise of the writer. Motivational experts John-Roger and Peter McWilliams tell us that we are actually constructed in such a way that we will be successful.[2] Educational consultants Brian Tracy and Bettie Young say that we contain the power to achieve.[3] Psychologists Muriel James and Dorothy Jongeward insist that each of us enters life with the ability to win.[4] Ex-lawyer Arnold M. Patent says our natural state is one of abundance.[5] Sales trainer Og Mandino insists that he (and, I suppose, by implication, all human beings, as well) is nature's greatest miracle.[6] Mind-power advocates Irving Oyle and Susan Jean tell us that we are all brilliant and live amidst abundance.[7] And philosopher Tom Morris advises us to become the people we can be.[8]

Are we born to greatness? Is abundance our natural state, or is it just another lie of the self-help movement? I think the answer lies quite simply with the message itself, if we analyze it logically.

First, we must understand what we mean when we say "people are born to" or "our natural state" or "the nature of man." What we are talking about are essential characteristics and qualities. For something to be an essential characteristic of an object, it must be inherent in that object, a basic and indispensable part. When we say that it is the nature of diamonds to be hard, we are saying that hardness is an essential characteristic of diamonds, that diamonds cannot be other than hard. A soft diamond could not exist because it wouldn't be a diamond if it were soft. A soft diamond is a logical contradiction, and such contradictions are untrue. Furthermore, when we say that an essential characteristic of diamonds is hardness, we are saying that diamonds do not need to "learn" hardness or "practice" hardness principles or have hardness "uncovered" in them. They are diamonds, and so they are hard.

But this is exactly what self-help writers do not say, because they cannot, about human beings. They cannot say that our natural state is abundance, or that we are naturally great, and therefore we *are* abundance, we *are* greatness. To make such a statement would be to imply that people who do not have abundance are not, by definition, human.

Worse, by making such a statement, self-help writers would put themselves out of business. If we are, in our essential nature, great, then we don't need self-help books to learn how to unlock greatness or practice the abundant life. But this is precisely what self-help writers continue to tell us, in defiance of all logic. They insist that we need to *learn* how to be all the things they say we are by *nature*. Brian Tracy, for example, says that his book will teach readers how to unlock their greatness potential.[9]

The same sort of statement is made by most other self-help

writers, including the religious ones. Norman Vincent Peale tells us that we can be the winners God made us by unlocking our plus factor. Schuller says we just need to practice possibility thinking to be winners. But if greatness really were a part of our essential nature, none of that advice would be necessary. No one would have to tell us *how* to be winners. We would just win.

In addition to its logical problems, the assertion that men and women are born to greatness is belied by our personal and collective experience. Human history is a dismal litany of wars, brutalities, atrocities, injustices, pain, and failure. Judging from what we know of our past and present behaviors and what we can anticipate of our future, it seems that the essential nature of human beings is predatory and animalistic.

There is, of course, another whole aspect to this lie of universal human greatness. It's just plain silly. Can everyone be a king? Who would be the subjects? And what of different gifts and abilities? I have known children who are truly born musicians. You cannot stop their music from coming out. I have also known children who could not make music if their lives depended on it, and only constant rewards and punishments could make them even marginally competent on a musical instrument. In the same way, some children are intellectually or artistically or athletically or interpersonally gifted. Most of the rest of us are just plain ordinary.

And what about greatness? Isn't it really a matter of comparison? If we are all great, how is great defined? Look up the word great in just about any dictionary, and you will find definitions such as outstanding, superior, eminent, and distinguished. These words all imply some sort of comparison. You cannot be outstanding unless there is a common group from which you stand out. (I am reminded of a line from the Gilbert and Sullivan operetta *The Gondoliers*. "When everybody is somebody, then no one's anybody!") What self-help authors really mean when they say that everyone is born to be great is that you, who are reading their book and putting their program into action, will become greater than the people who don't take advantage of this wonderful opportunity. But that is a very different matter altogether.

ORIGIN OF THE LIE

The ugly duckling who becomes a swan, the frog who is really an enchanted prince, the dragon masquerading as an old peasant man, the heir to the throne dressed in rag-picker's clothes, the god disguised as a street urchin. These stories or others like them are known in every culture around the world. Humans cling to the belief that if we could just scrape away our common or vulgar exterior, we would be revealed for the glorious beings we are.

Where did it come from, this longing to reveal a greatness that we obviously don't possess? Why do we want to believe that we're born to win, born to be rich, born to succeed? I believe that this longing has a dual origin. It is, in some small measure, born of a deeply buried awareness, a collective and ancient human memory, of what men and women were created to be. But we traded that greatness, in what must surely be the worst bargain of all time, for a spurious sense of autonomy.

In a larger measure, I think that our longing for greatness springs from our experience of God and our distorted reaction to that experience, which resulted in the Fall. We know that greatness is an essential characteristic of God. He *is* Greatness. We see His greatness, although dimly, through the sin that clouds our vision. We see it, and we want it for ourselves, because we want to be like God. We want to be God. Positive self-talk trainer Shad Helmstetter tells us that we are everything, as limitless as the universe.[10] What is this but a declaration of divinity? Always while this earth lasts, human beings will repeat the sin of Adam and Eve and insist on their own godhood. At its heart, that is what the entire self-help movement is about. Its origin is the sin of the Fall; its lies are the lies of Satan.

CONSEQUENCES OF THE LIE

The veneration of visible greatness

We are, as the old hymn reminds us, frail children of dust and feeble as frail. We long to be great, but in our frailty we settle for the cheap goods of this world, the goods that are no less dust than we are ourselves. We venerate the shallow, the material, the visible. We are seduced by the greatness of wealth and success and power and fame—visible greatness. To be great in human terms is to be *seen* to be great. If no one acknowledges our greatness, how can we be sure that we are great? Because we must be recognized for our accomplishments, the success programs we follow, the self-help writers we believe are those that produce *material* results. We will get the job promotion or the pay raise or the beautiful lover. We will live in the best neighborhoods and wear the right clothes and read the hip books and align ourselves with the popular causes.

Contempt for failure

Because we venerate visible greatness, we denigrate failure. More than that, we are often openly hostile to and contemptuous of people who prove to be failures. We distance ourselves from the poor, the infirm, the losers. Worse, we often blame them for their condition. Their failure is proof of a character flaw. After all, if humans are born to greatness, if the natural state of man is abundance, then these ignoble people must have perverted their natural course in some way. They must have debased their royal heritage.

This contempt for failure has spawned a kind of caste system in America. In the formal Hindu caste system of India, membership in a low caste is a kind of punishment for sins in past lives. People deserved to be Sudras or, worse, Untouchables and outside of the caste system altogether. (The caste system is one of the reasons that Christian conversion remains uncommon in India, where Christ's suffering and death is considered a mark of past sins. Christ, in the Indian way of thinking, deserved what He got.)

While we have no formal caste system in America, there is a tacitly accepted belief that poverty is the result of laziness and wickedness. Poor people deserve their poverty. We see this belief acted out in the almost tangible hatred with which many Americans, including Christians, view the welfare system. We forget the Biblical mandate to welcome the strangers, care for the widows and orphans, feed the poor, tend the sick, visit the prisoners. These people are trying to take advantage of us, trying to cheat us out of what is rightfully ours, the material success we worked so hard for. They could be successful if they wanted to, we reason. Their impoverished external circumstances must result from an impoverished internal life. So we are able to walk past the homeless on our city streets, not only offering no help, but not even seeing them. They are the throw-away people, these failures who belie our belief in man's greatness.

The cult of the hero

In *Living Above the Level of Mediocrity*, Chuck Swindoll tells the story of a man who overcame rickets, poverty, a ghetto upbringing, and a juvenile arrest record to become wealthy and famous. This man is held up as an example to us, as Swindoll recounts the wonders of his impressive house in an exclusive neighborhood, his luxurious car, his elegant offices, his glamorous life among the wealthy and powerful. This man found the greatness within himself, Swindoll tells us, to soar with the eagles. Who is this man? Orenthal James Simpson, a man Swindoll describes as refined and strong enough to be gentle.[11]

What do we know about O. J. Simpson today? He is a man so given to violence against his wife that he was arrested and prosecuted for her murder. And whether we believe him guilty or not, evidence presented at his trial strongly suggests that he beat his wife repeatedly while married to her, that he humiliated her in public, and that he stalked her after their divorce. Furthermore, when called to task for his spousal abuse, he showed contempt for our judicial system. But he was O. J. Simpson, American hero, the man who released the abundance within himself, and he did not have to answer to the authority that governs common folk.

The O. J. Simpson story is typical of the trap we fall into when we measure greatness by worldly standards, when we lose our capacity to venerate all but the visible. We create a cult of heroes who live out for us what we can only dream for ourselves. Would Swindoll have told Simpson's story in such glowing terms if O. J. had remained in the ghetto, obscure and poor, but a man who practiced a righteous walk with God?

The heroes of self-help, the heroes of America, are people who have risen from poverty to fame and wealth, usually through sports, entertainment, or politics. We identify with them because of their humble origins, and we hold to the hope that maybe we will become great, too. And so we lionize figures like Mike Tyson and Michael Jackson, Jim Bakker and Jimmy Swaggart. And then something happens. The great hero, the god-man, is exposed as weak and sinful and corrupt, just like all of us. But like Greek tragedy, his fall is greater than ours, because he has farther to fall. Despite what we would like to believe, the hero is not great; he is human. And to be human is to be very wicked indeed.

WHAT THE BIBLE SAYS ABOUT MANKIND'S NATURAL CONDITION

A recurring theme of the Bible, particularly of the Old Testament, is the greatness of God. My favorite of these passages is Psalm 145, a majestic song of praise in which David declares, "Great is the LORD, and greatly to be praised; and his greatness is unsearchable."[12] The *New International Version* says that God's greatness cannot be fathomed. Unsearchable. Unfathomable. These words mean more than our inability to understand God's greatness. They mean that God's greatness is so enormous that we cannot even measure it, get to its depth, chart its boundaries, find its extent, or comprehend its size—because it is infinite. And we, the finite, cannot even begin to hold the infinite, even in our imaginations.

The Bible also speaks of the greatness of Christ: "Therefore God exalted him to the highest place and gave him the name that is above every name, that at the name of Jesus every knee should bow, in heaven and on earth and under the earth, and every tongue confess that Jesus Christ is Lord, to the glory of God the Father."[13] John the Baptist, himself acknowledged as a man of God, recognized the supreme greatness of Jesus, a man "the thongs of whose sandals I am not worthy to stoop down and untie."[14] Another prophet foretold Jesus' greatness: "Therefore I will give him a portion among the great, and he will divide the spoils with the strong, because he poured out his life unto death, and was numbered with the transgressors. For he bore the sin of many, and made intercession for the transgressors."[15]

Greatness is part of God's essential nature, part of His glory as God the Son. But what of men and women? Are we really born to greatness, born to win, as the success writers insist? Not if we believe Scripture. In fact, the Bible has something very different to say about mankind.

People are sinful.

First, the Bible tells us that each person's nature, right from the start of life, is one of sin and rebellion. "Surely I was sinful at birth, sinful from the time my mother conceived me," the psalmist wrote.[16] The writer of Job, recognizing man's sinful nature, asked, "How can one born of woman be pure?"[17] "What is man, that he could be pure, or one born of woman, that he could be righteous?"[18] In Jeremiah we read, "The heart is deceitful above all things, and desperately wicked: who can know it?"[19] And Paul reminds us that "all have sinned and fall short of the glory of God."[20]

People are slaves.

Second, the Bible tells us that because of our sin, we are born slaves. We are held in bondage to sin, and our ultimate fate is physical death and corruption. Paul describes this condition of human life, confessing, "I am unspiritual, sold as a slave to sin."[21] Paul makes clear what the result of that sin is when he tells us that "the wages of sin is death."[22]

I do not think it is a coincidence that God chose to reveal Himself to the world through a slave people or that Jewish tradition places so much emphasis on God's miraculous act in freeing the Hebrews from slavery. This story is a pre-echo of God's even more astonishing act of redemption on the Cross. In the Old Testament, it took the death of the first-born of Egypt to free the Hebrew slaves. In the New Testament, it took the death of God's first-born to free all of us from sin-imposed slavery.

People are dust.

Third, we know that mankind is merely dust. "The LORD God formed the man from the dust of the ground."[23] Because of his sin, man was condemned to work the earth from which he was formed and then return to it in his death. "By the sweat of your brow you will eat your food until you return to the ground, since from it you were taken; for dust you are and to dust you will return."[24]

People are insignificant.

Fourth, we know that we are of little consequence, passing through time so quickly that our presence can make hardly a ripple on the vast ocean of eternity. David marvels that God should even be interested in such creatures. "O LORD, what is man that you care for him, the son of man that you think of him? Man is like a breath; his days are like a fleeting shadow," sings David, acknowledging both man's insignificance and God's graciousness.[25] Clearly, David understood that human beings are nothing in themselves. God infuses them with meaning—not for their sake, but for God's own sake.

People suffer.

Finally, people are born not to greatness, but to pain and suffering. "Yet man is born to trouble as surely as sparks fly upward," the writer of Job tells us.[26] It doesn't take most of us too many years on this earth to experience the truth of this statement for ourselves, no matter how much we would like to deny it. Not long ago, I had occasion to speak with a man who was astonished by an accident involving a member of his family. This man was wealthy and successful. He saw himself as favored in God's eyes, and he did not understand how something bad could happen to anyone connected with him. I told him that no one is immune to suffering. Six months later, this man was diagnosed with inoperable stomach cancer, and three months after that, he was dead.

The premise that man's natural state is one of greatness illustrates perhaps better than any other assertion of the self-help movement that fallen people are on a "journey homeward to habitual self."[27] That journey must inevitably lead away from God. But isn't that Satan's intention? Isn't that what lies behind the self-help movement: the construction of a relationship with myself, built with the rubble of my demolished relationship with God?

It was not always so. There must have been a time, before the Fall, when humankind was intimately connected to God and when man and woman were very great indeed. Of course, even that greatness was a reflection of God. C. S. Lewis imagines that time: "In perfect cyclic movement, being, power and joy descended from God to man in the form of gift and returned from man to God in the form of obedient love and ecstatic adoration: and in this sense, though not in all, man was then truly the son of God, the prototype of Christ, perfectly enacting in joy and ease of all the faculties and all the senses that filial self-surrender which our Lord enacted in the agonies of the crucifixion."[28]

Now we have no choice but to face life without this greatness. The closest we can ever come to greatness here on earth is through our daily abortive attempts to die to self and live in Christ. At least we have the hope, the consolation, the privilege of knowing that God is making the journey back to Himself with us and even for us. Apart from this relationship, we have no greatness, no glory, no abundance—only death.

7

Lie Four:
I Can Be As Successful
As I Want, If Only . . .

In the prologue to his 1954 book, *The Self-Made Man in America*, Irvin G. Wyllie wrote:

> The principal American aspiration could be expressed by the single word *Success*. But what is success? Politicians equate it with power, publicists with fame. Teachers and moralists rate themselves successful when they have influenced the minds and characters of others. Men of creative instinct strive for self-realization. Humanitarians identify success with service, reformers with the alteration of the social order. To the devout, success is salvation, and to thousands of plain people it is nothing more than contentment and a sense of happiness. Each of these definitions embodies worthy ideals, and all have their champions. But no one of these concepts enjoys such universal favor in America as that which equates success with making money.[1]

Things haven't really changed since Wyllie's day. While we still equate success with various accomplishments, depending upon our interests, most of us use money as the benchmark for true success. ("If you're so smart, why ain't you rich?") And today's success books, whatever other forms of success they may be about and however spiritual or psychological a spin they may put on their message, continue to equate wealth with success.

Millionaire entrepreneur and success guru Charles Givens asserts that the desire for money—at least enough to realize our dreams—is universal. He also recommends his three number-one best-selling books as useful manuals for consistent financial success.[2] In her success book, *Having It All,* Helen Gurley Brown promises that her readers will make money if they follow her principles, which include detailed sexual advice.[3] Goddess writer Terry Cole-Whittaker says that if we work at something we love and do an excellent job at it, money will follow.[4] Robert J. Ringer, in *Looking Out for #1,* observes that everybody cares about making money.[5] Success consultant Leo Weidner tells his clients that every person is born to have wealth.[6] And the granddaddy of them all, Napoleon Hill, tells us to imagine ourselves as millionaires.[7]

This correspondence of wealth and success figures prominently in the numerous folksy stories success books use to illustrate or to prove the validity of their advice. These anecdotes are, almost without exception, about wealthy people, individuals who have realized their deepest dreams and, in the process, become incredibly rich. Typically these books serve up a monotonous fare of stories about Sam Walton or Bill Cosby or Mary Kay or Lee Iacocca or some other cultural icon. But they also include stories of "regular" people who, while not necessarily achieving fame, nevertheless attain considerable material comfort by following the books' success principles. Typical are the insurance salesman who more than quadrupled his income after ten months on a personal success program or the computer programmer who gained the courage to open his own company and is now on his way to becoming a millionaire. But I'm sure you've heard or read similar stories. They are the lure that keeps people buying success books, attending success seminars and motivational lectures, investing their savings in get-rich schemes.

Without a doubt, success books are about personal wealth. And there is money to be made from such books—for the writers, the agents, and the publishing industry. Stephen Covey and Anthony Robbins, for example, have each managed to turn one bestseller into several bestsellers by coming up with a newer and catchier title, changing the spin on their message slightly, and adding some new examples. Both of these success writers, in a stroke of marketing genius, have reissued their success manuals as affirmation books. Covey's *The 7 Habits of Highly Successful People* has reappeared in the little affirmation book *Daily Reflections for Highly Effective People.* Tony Robbins's *Unlimited Power* has made a fresh appearance (U.S. paperback retail price $10.00) as *Giant Steps: 365 Daily Lessons in Self-Mastery.* Robert J. Ringer has managed to produce four books with the same message as, and on the strength of, his first big seller, *Million Dollar Habits.*

What about the reader? Will he really become rich or successful? Does he get anything at all? Or does he find himself, like Arlo Guthrie in *"Alice's Restaurant Massacree,"* having to pay fifty dollars and pick up the garbage? I can't help but wonder. After all, if success books are—not to put too fine a point on it—successful, why do so many people continue to buy one after the other? Shouldn't the first one have done the trick? Why do publishers keep issuing new ones? Why do writers keep thumbing their thesauruses, looking for new ways to restate the same old cliches? If these books work, shouldn't there be far more wealthy, contented, fulfilled, and successful people in America today?

As you've probably guessed by now, all of this leads me to the next lie of the self-help movement: the lie of success. This lie tells us that we can have anything, do anything, be anything, that we can achieve all of our dreams in both our personal and professional lives *if* we follow the formula or plan or secrets or guidelines set forth in the success books. Each time a new book is published, its author promises the reader that *this time* he'll be successful; *this time* he'll hear the magic words or the secret formula that will unlock the portals of success; *this time* he will be able to translate the plan into reality.

In *SuperSelf*, Givens offers just such a guarantee, telling readers that his success strategies are so foolproof that any possibility of failure has been eliminated. Givens also asserts that his strategies represent a brand-new approach to a successful life.[8] And just what does Givens's brand-new approach include?

Develop a blueprint.

Discover your dreams.

Write down your goals.

Align your goals with your values.

Develop an action plan.

Prioritize your activities.

Practice self-discipline and good time management.

Eliminate interruptions.

Learn how to handle stress and get enough rest.

I don't know about you, but I find Givens's advice somewhat less than revolutionary. Almost exactly the same how-to-be-successful formula appears in just about every success book on the market today. Of course, the different writers may emphasize one piece of advice over another. Or they may use different terms, say "picturizing" rather than "positive visualization," or "happy thoughts" rather than "positive mental attitude," or "definite major purpose" rather than "white-hot goal." They may favor psychological jargon or business idioms or computer slang. They may have a different number of success "steps." (Covey has seven habits; Tony Robbins has five keys.) Or they may, like Robert Ringer, even deny that there is a success secret before they go on to provide the simple techniques that will ensure that success is ours. Despite these minor differences, the advice of success authors from Tony Robbins to Stephen Covey to Zig

Ziglar to Og Mandino to Dennis Waitley is mind-numbingly similar.

Not only isn't Givens's success advice original, but his insistence—more than that, his guarantee—that we will be successful *if* we follow his advice isn't new. Nearly every one of the dozens of success books I have read makes a similar claim. In *Achieving the Balance,* personal success "coach" Leo Weidner says that following his plan will finally allow readers to achieve the goals that have eluded them in the past. Robert Ringer says all his readers will be financially successful. How? By practicing rational thinking, self-discipline, and Ringer's success principles.[9]

Quite apart from its lack of originality, Givens's advice, like that of the other success writers, is overly secular and egocentric—from a Christian point of view. He tells us to eliminate interruptions. But what if the annoying interruption in my success-filled day is just exactly the work that God has called me to do for that day? Maybe it is as trivial (to me) as having a long and boring telephone conversation with a neighbor who is lonely. And what about the time-management advice? Is my time really mine to manage? And how about those goals and values? Shouldn't I be trying to discover *God's* goals for me, not my goals for myself? As for values, well, as a Christian, I ought already to be clear about the values that God has called me to affirm and defend. I don't need to find my own values. And what's all this talk about priorities? I thought Jesus settled that issue once and for all when He told us to seek God's kingdom first.[10]

Sadly, the Christian market is also full of success books, perfect examples of the distortion whereby many Christians strive to be "of the world" but not "in the world." This is the same disturbing trend that has spawned megachurches founded specifically to "meet people where they are" or "offer people something practical in their lives." (Apparently the Gospel is not enough.) These churches provide aerobics classes, fashion and beauty lectures, weight-loss programs, investment seminars, tax preparation courses, self-esteem classes, weight rooms and racquetball courts, live theater—everything the world provides without the world's taint of sin, without rubbing shoulders with the damned.

The Christian version of success provides the same monetary rewards as the secular version, the same opulent lifestyle, the same opportunities to rub elbows with the powerful and famous. But it does so with the external trappings of pop Christianity, telling us that God wants to show us how to become financially successful, giving us permission to indulge our greed. This marriage of material success and Christianity has been a part of the American religious scene for some time. Wyllie noted that a striking feature of the nineteenth-century success/self-help movement is that so many of its leaders were clergymen. "By teaching that godliness was in league with riches such spokesmen put the sanction of the church on the get-ahead values of the business community. And by so teaching they encouraged each rising generation to believe that it was possible to serve both God and Mammon."[11] In our century, these themes are repeated and reinforced in the work of such writers as Norman Vincent Peale, Robert Schuller, Pat Robertson, Og Mandino, Zig Ziglar, and Florence Littauer. Many evangelical publishing houses, such as Word and Thomas Nelson, continue to deliver a regular fare of books on financial success, money management, investment strategies, and business growth—giving Christians the clear impression that God wants us to be wealthy and successful.

Even Jesus' conduct of His earthly ministry has been distorted to serve the purposes of success purveyors. An early example is the 1925 best-selling book *The Man Nobody Knows*. Written by Bruce Barton, the son of a Congregationalist minister, the book portrayed Jesus as an aggressive modern businessman who knew how to organize and advertise.[12] Almost seventy years later, motivational speaker Mike Murdock echoes those same themes in his *One-Minute Businessman's Devotional*. In it, Murdock presents Jesus as a kind of super-salesman, who, for example, believed in His product, knew how to ask the right questions, and stayed in the center of what He knew best.[13] I would find Murdock's assertions amusing if they weren't almost blasphemous. Jesus didn't need to *ask* people what they desired; He *knew*. And He certainly didn't *ask* people what they needed; He *told* them. His was the authority of Creator dealing with creature, not businessman dealing with customer. Jesus didn't need to *stay* in the center of anything, because He *was* the center of everything. He was and is and will ever be the source and the reason for all that exists. His expertise is everything, because everything is made by Him and through Him and for Him.

ORIGIN OF THE LIE

The lie of success, which tells me that I will be successful if I follow certain plans, contains within it a deeper lie. This is the lie that tells me I *should* be successful, that I both *deserve* and *need* success. So fundamental is this lie that it is seldom even stated in success books; the writers assume that we all agree that success is a fitting and necessary goal for human beings. It is the lie that fuels our credit card industry, that is fed by and feeds on a culture of instant gratification. But where did this lie come from?

The need for success, whether measured in wealth or accomplishment, is part and parcel of the human desire to control a world that seems irrational, unpredictable, and frightening. My success keeps me safe and comfortable in an uncertain universe. Thomas Howard has written about C. S. Lewis's treatment of this theme in *Perelandra*, in which Venus's first man and woman have been forbidden to live on fixed land, but must remain on floating islands. Tor and Tinidril, Howard explains, "must learn first that their real safety lies, not in apparent fixity and motionlessness and predictability, but rather in the Will of Maleldil [i.e. God]. To insist on an obvious fixity . . . is like amassing money: all are ways of shoring up against contingency and unpredictability."[14] We are afraid to trust in God, so we trust in our own success, our own wealth, to protect and save us.

More than that, the trust we humans place in our success and wealth shows that we want to call all the shots in our lives. Success writer Robert Ringer admits that money is important because it can buy freedom.[15] Freedom may be the holiest word in the American vocabulary. It is the ultimate good to Americans, secular and Christian. But freedom means that we can order our lives on our own terms rather than on God's terms.

This desire to be free, to be in charge of ourselves, results from pride, the sin that C. S. Lewis has called "the complete anti-God state of mind."[16] Pride permeates the success movement, in which competition and comparison, two hallmarks of pride, figure prominently. Competition and comparison are essential because, after all, wealth can't really be wealth if everyone has as much money as I do. And success isn't really success if everyone achieves just as much as I do. "Pride gets no pleasure out of having something, only out of having more of it than the next man," says Lewis.[17] "Pride always means enmity—it is enmity. And not only enmity between man and man, but enmity to God."[18] This is the legacy of the serpent's lie. Eve believed that lie, and now her children scrabble around in desperation, seeking wealth and success, trying to prove their greatness, their godness.

CONSEQUENCES OF THE LIE

Self-absorption

Like all the lies of the self-help movement, the lie of success places our focus on ourselves and encourages us to put ourselves first. But this is not the self-absorption of self-esteem, which tells us that if we love ourselves first, we'll be better able to love other people. Nor is it the message of happiness, which tells us that we'll be better able to serve others if we first make ourselves happy. No, this is the self-absorption of the "I" that Pascal calls hateful, the ego that "assumes its self-sufficiency and self-mastery and imagines itself secure against all vicissitudes."[19] This is the self-absorption that denies "the thing undergirding all possibility of civil human life, namely the recognition of the prior claim that the other person has on your own claim to yourself."[20]

The self-absorption preached by success writers tells me that the most important thing in my life is that I believe in myself. One such writer calls it my creed, which is a written statement that includes everything I desire and believe about myself.[21] Another writer shrouds this emphasis on self-absorption in the more lofty sounding term self-knowledge, which he says will set us free.[22] I thought it was Truth, in the person of Jesus Christ, that set us free.

Dehumanization of other people

When you deny that other people have a greater claim on you than you have on yourself, then you can simply discard people who are inconvenient or unhelpful or negative in some way. By the same token, you are free to use people who can help you achieve success. Either way, what you are doing is dehumanizing your fellow men and women. For example, Les Brown, an African-American motivational speaker and success writer, tells us that we should avoid relationships that undermine our goals. We should associate only with people who will enrich and empower us, Brown says.[23]

Somewhat less blatant, but still making the point that we should associate with the rich and powerful, is Zig Ziglar's passage from *Over the Top* in which he congratulates himself for having appeared with outstanding Americans, such as Norman Vincent Peale, Ronald Reagan, Art Linkletter, Paul Harvey, W. Clement Stone, and Pat Boone.[24] Outstanding in what way? By whose judgment? Certainly, all these people are successful, wealthy, and famous. Does that make them any more valuable as associates than the trash collector or the grocery store cashier or the garrulous old man down the street?

Jesus appeared with a Samaritan woman, a prostitute, a tax collector, and blue-collar workers. When He wanted a break from His heavy preaching schedule, He spent time with two unimportant and unknown housewives. His association with the rich and powerful of His day generally resulted in exchanges that were not to the credit of those men who were successful according to the world's standards. And what about God's choice of a slave nation to carry His message to the world and a peasant woman to carry His Son?

Of course, it is true that we all know people whose company seems to make us less than we are and others in whose company we become more. But when we seek out people specifically for the experience of self-fulfillment or self-aggrandizement, we are well on the way to using people as things.

Faith in magic

Religion teaches us to glorify God. But when we stop glorifying God and start using Him, religion becomes magic. A striking feature of religious success books is that prayer, Bible study, and religious observances become a means to gain mastery and success in worldly terms. In their review of religious success literature, Schneider and Dornbusch conclude, "There is a heavy emphasis that religion brings all kinds of things that are 'good' from a human point of view—success and life-mastery, power to live by, wealth or happiness, and the like."[25] Os Guinness has also observed that "prosperity as providence" is basic in American religious life.[26] We believe that God—providence, if you will—has as His special plan the prosperity of America.

The cult of Christian magic with its emphasis on the usefulness of God is blatantly illustrated in the 1930s work of Emmet Fox, who asserted that by doing the work that God intends for us to do, we will be rewarded monetarily, and we will be gloriously happy.[27] This is a far cry from Paul's reminder to the early Christians that "all who desire to live godly in Christ Jesus will be persecuted,"[28] but is quite in line with the work of Norman Vincent Peale, who told us that Christianity is entirely practical and that we have enough power to blow up New York City if we want to use it. Not only did Peale believe that Christianity is practical, but he even gave precise spiritual methodologies whereby Christians could tap in to the power of prayer. Peale believed that Christianity could be reduced to precise formulas. By applying those formulas, we would see our religion work in amazing ways.[29]

More recently the authors of a Bible study guide called *Alive!* insisted that they want to help Christians tap "the tremendous resources available in Jesus Christ."[30] TV evangelist Pat Robertson claims that God's principles produce prosperity. And business speaker Mike Murdock says that he has been able to uncover the Scriptures' success laws. Murdock recommends Bible reading and prayer as success generators, insisting that our best ideas will appear when we enter God's presence.[31] C. S. Lewis had something rather different to say about the presence of God: "The real test of being in the presence of God is that you either forget about yourself altogether or see yourself as a small, dirty object. It is better to forget about yourself altogether."[32]

Distorted values

Perhaps the most obvious consequence of the success lie is a distortion or, worse, an absolute destruction of our values. Even the most casual cultural observer can see the overwhelming role that success and material acquisition play in American life. Despite the fact that the United States is the most church-going, the most overtly religious of the Western nations, we are a society that is often ridiculed and scorned by the rest of the world for our blatant materialism. And who can blame other nations for their assessment? After all, it is our own success experts, writers such as Charles Givens, Mike Murdock, and Robert Ringer, who tell us that we can have it all, that God cares about money, and that money is freedom.

The result of these distorted values can even be seen in the lives of some of America's most popular evangelists. Pat

Robertson, for example, lives the lifestyle of old money in a walled estate on professionally manicured grounds dotted with carefully replicated and tastefully decorated colonial-style brick buildings. What kind of witness is this to a world that knows mostly hunger, poverty, and disease?

WHAT THE BIBLE SAYS ABOUT HUMAN ACCOMPLISHMENT

The story of God's revelation of His essential nature to mankind, recorded in the Bible, is a story that belies all human ideas of value, achievement, success, and prosperity. (But then, the wisdom of God and the wisdom of this world are two very different things.) Throughout the Old Testament, God pursues a tribe of slave people, always keeping His promises despite their constant disobedience.

In the New Testament, He walks away from glory and is born a human baby to a peasant woman in a country occupied by hostile, foreign, pagan troops. As a human being, He consorts with the dregs of society and submits to "the worst form of criminal death, the supreme Roman penalty, inflicted only on the lower classes and slaves," a death so terrible that "even talk of it could evoke horror."[33] As a resurrected God, "He stoops to conquer, He will have us even though we have shown that we prefer everything else to Him, and come to Him, because there is 'nothing better' now to be had. . . . It is hardly complimentary to God that we should choose Him as an alternative to Hell: yet even this He accepts."[34]

The humility of God is, to me, the most amazing miracle. It has worked throughout human history to show us how we are to act toward ourselves, toward one another, and toward our Creator. It does not tell me to seek my own wealth or success or self-aggrandizement. It tells me to empty myself of self.

Religious success writers would have us believe that God wants us to be happy and prosperous. But the Bible tells us that

God wants us to be holy, to be righteous, to be creatures worthy of His love. Becoming such a creature does not involve worldly success; it involves submission, suffering, and death. Jesus Himself tells us, "If anyone would come after me, he must deny himself and take up his cross and follow me."[35] Jesus' hearers would have understood that to "take up his cross" meant "to carry the horizontal beam of the cross out to the site of execution, generally past a jeering mob. In rhetorically strong terms, Jesus describes what all true disciples must be ready for: if they follow him, they must be ready to face literal scorn and death, for they must follow him to the cross."[36]

This is a far cry from Mike Murdock's assertion that Jesus showed people how to be financially successful.[37] When Jesus calls us to discipleship, He does not call us to worldly success. He calls us to come and die. It is the call to obedience, and often times that obedience means poverty, persecution, and grief. But, as Puddleglum aptly observed in C. S. Lewis's *The Silver Chair*, "You see, Aslan didn't tell Pole what would happen. He only told her what to do. That fellow may be the death of us once he's up, I shouldn't wonder. But that doesn't let us off following the Sign."[38] Puddleglum knew that obedience to Aslan (the Christ figure in Lewis's world of Narnia) might not be safe, but that was no excuse for not obeying him. And Jesus does not guarantee success or happiness or comfort when we follow Him. In fact, He told us we can expect some pretty terrible things to happen, at least in this life. But whatever the consequences, our call to obedience must stand. We either obey or we go our own way. We can't excuse our lack of obedience by saying that Jesus never meant for us to be poor or unhappy.

Paul, too, taught us in no uncertain terms that if we expect to share Christ's glory, we can also expect to share His suffering. "Now if we are children, then we are heirs—heirs of God and co-heirs with Christ, if indeed we share in his sufferings in order that we may also share in his glory."[39] But not only is suffering expected of Christians, it is a *privilege* for Christians. "For it has been granted to you on behalf of Christ not only to believe on him, but also to suffer for him."[40] And Peter tells us that we should rejoice in that suffering. "But rejoice that you participate in the sufferings of Christ, so that you may be overjoyed when his glory is revealed."[41]

And what of the accomplishments that success books tell us we attain through our own efforts, through goal-setting and prioritizing and time management and perseverance? It is all illusion, the Scriptures make clear, telling us that everything we have is a gift of God, that He sends prosperity and calamity where and to whom He will. God is sovereign, despite what we may like to believe about ourselves. He works out His plan for us in the way that He knows is best. And for Christians that plan means that God will test us and purify us with the refiner's fire. Because in the end, God knows what we must struggle so hard to learn, namely that it profits us nothing to gain the whole world—success, fame, wealth, pleasure—and lose our own souls.

8

Lie Five:
I Need to Build
My Self-Esteem

Crime and violence, alcoholism and drug use, teenage pregnancy, child and spouse abuse, chronic welfare dependence, school failure, divorce, discrimination, suicide. Name any social ill or personal problem, and you will find a host of experts who point to the same cause—low self-esteem. So pervasive is this belief in the importance of self-esteem that the California legislature has even created a Task Force to Promote Self-Esteem and Personal and Social Responsibility. And in a recent issue of *Entrepreneur* magazine, business consultant and futurist Edith Weiner suggested that promoting self-esteem was good for business. Her advice to entrepreneurs includes finding ways to make their products and services desirable for bolstering customers' well-being and self-esteem.[1] I can think of no more convincing measure of an idea's popularity in America than that it be touted as a marketing tool.

The need to feel good about oneself, to love oneself, to build one's self-esteem is not only accepted almost without question in our culture, but it is even offered as a basic human birthright. Self-esteem experts, such as psychotherapist Nathaniel Branden, who heads the Branden Institute for Self-Esteem, tell us that as human beings, we have the right to love ourselves. Without this self-love, they say, we are doomed to lead lives of failure and misery. According to a business training video from the Barksdale Foundation, low self-esteem costs lives and money, while a recent article in a popular women's magazine asserted that low self-esteem is a major cause of depression, particularly in women.[2]

New Age guru Shirley MacLaine sounds an even more cosmic warning about the danger of low self-esteem, saying that many of our modern horrors result from a lack of self-love.[3] Those horrors include environmental pollution, wars, famine, and disease. And lest one get the impression that only the secular world is in danger from the damage of low self-esteem, former missionary and pastor David A. Seamands says that many Christians suffer from feelings of low self-esteem and that they regularly belittle themselves.[4]

The fifth lie of the self-help movement, the lie of self-esteem, attempts to convince us that human ills result not from a broken relationship with God, not from sin, but from a broken relationship with the self. Once that relationship is healed, according to the lie, we are free to lead lives of happiness and fulfillment, serving others as well as ourselves. And how do we heal our broken relationship with the self? By building our self-esteem.

But just what does self-esteem mean? Interestingly, experts don't necessarily agree. Some writers keep the definition simple and call it self-love. Others take a more complicated approach, claiming that self-esteem is the ability to trust your own mind and to know that you are worthy of happiness. (This writer does not, however, tell us what he means by happiness.) Other definitions involve having a positive self-image, appreciating your own worth and importance, and liking and respecting yourself whether you win or lose. (What winning and losing involve is not clear.)

The definition of self-esteem is not its only fuzzy aspect. The means by which we are told we can achieve self-esteem are similarly confusing and often contradictory. Some experts contend that we develop self-esteem when our parents love and accept us unconditionally. In this view, self-esteem is a function of how well we are treated at an early age. We can no more choose to develop self-esteem than we can choose to grow. If we are physically nourished, our bodies grow. If we are emotionally fed, our self-esteem grows. Other experts argue that self-esteem is not passive, not given to us by others, but is acquired over time; it is something we develop through our own behaviors and the feedback we get from them.

Experts also disagree on how much self-esteem is enough. Most psychologists insist that no one can have too much self-esteem, which is seen as the glue that holds the personality together, making us kind and understanding of others and allowing us to interact socially without feeling threatened. People who brag, who constantly assert their own rights, who compare themselves to others to show their superiority, really suffer from low self-esteem, these psychologists say. If such people were really secure in themselves, they wouldn't need to put themselves first. On the other side of this argument are psychologists who claim that too much self-esteem can lead to arrogant, self-centered, and disrespectful behavior. When taken to its extreme, self-esteem becomes a narcissistic personality disorder, these psychologists say.[5]

Confusing definitions aside, what happens to people who are lucky enough to have self-esteem or to develop self-esteem? Do they really lead the wonderful lives promised them? Not necessarily. No matter how successful many people become, they remain dissatisfied with themselves. In a study of people who suffered from what has been dubbed the imposter phenomenon, clinical psychologist Joan C. Harvey looked at people who feared being exposed as fakes, despite their tremendous success.[6] These people, she found, score very high on the Rosenberg Scale, which measures self-esteem. By both material and psychological standards, they should be happy. Instead, they live in constant fear and dissatisfaction.

Despite all the confusion and despite the documented failure of self-esteem to live up to its advertising, most people today are convinced that building self-esteem will solve personal and societal problems. So entrenched is this belief that self-esteem courses have become standard fare in American schools, where self-esteem is considered more important than intelligence as a predictor of performance.

Typical of self-esteem materials designed for public schools is the booklet *100 ways to enhance self-concept in the classroom*. Among the 100 suggestions for building self-esteem are keeping a feelings journal and writing an autobiography. (As the parent of a child who hates to write and says she can never think of anything to say when given a writing assignment, I can only wonder at suggestions that might lower the self-esteem of the nonwriters in the classroom.) This booklet also suggests mutual self-disclosure, fantasy sharing, bragging, a pride line, a personal flag, and a collage of the self, among other things. These exercises, according to the author, are designed to allow each student's private thoughts to be recognized as fit subject matter to share.[7] (But if a child's thoughts are shared, how can they be private?)

The booklet also suggests that students engage in a mantra session in which they chant aloud that they are worthwhile, no matter what anyone says.[8] This protestation of worthiness sounds to me an awful lot like a psychologically trendy version of, "Sticks and stones may break my bones, but names will never hurt me." That popular "mantra" of my childhood didn't work then, and I doubt that the self-esteem mantra works for today's children. The booklet also recommends that students engage in a values clarification exercise and answer questions about their families. The author does not explain, however, why teachers have the right to question children about their private lives and personal relationships.

A more recent example of self-esteem books for school children is *Honesty, Perseverance and Other Virtues: Using the 4 Conditions of Self-Esteem in Elementary and Middle Schools*.[9] This book is part of a recent trend to reintroduce virtues and personal responsibility into a culture that has been taught that there is no absolute right or wrong. The "favorite" virtues of the book's author include altruism, charity, compassion, courage, kindness, loyalty, perseverance, and trustworthiness. The book recommends that each week a virtue be chosen and activities planned around it, including essays, creative writing, news following, literature searches, plays, and art and community projects. The problem with this approach is that it fails to give children a context or a pretext for virtuous behavior. Children are taught to behave in socially acceptable or valuable ways because such behavior builds self-esteem, not because virtuous behaviors are valuable in themselves. And because self-esteem is made the goal, practicing virtue becomes self-serving.

The public school system has some excuse for its behavior. After all, it is a secular institution. It makes no pretense about recognizing any higher spiritual authority. But what excuse can there be for churches where self-esteem is replacing the Gospel? Michael P. Nichols, professor of psychiatry at Albany Medical College, lauds this trend in our churches, saying that pastors now speak about healthy self-esteem, giving their congregations sermons on wellness and wholism rather than quoting Scripture on the evils of the flesh.[10]

Of course, Nichols is on the outside looking in, so we can understand some of his misconceptions and distorted ideas about the message of Scriptures and the responsibility of the church. But what of an ostensibly Christian minister who influences the lives and thinking of tens of thousands of followers? What of people such as Robert Schuller, whose distortion of the Scriptures and the role of the church occurs not through ignorance but through deliberate manipulation? Schuller apparently wants to replace the Gospel of Jesus Christ with a gospel of self-esteem when he writes that the deepest need of human beings is not salvation from sin, if salvation means that the individual's self-esteem is assaulted.[11]

The gospel message in my Bible tells me in no uncertain terms that I am a sinner, but that I can be saved through the grace of God, which I do not deserve. It does not tell me that I am okay as I am or that I should learn to love myself in spite of my faults. If Schuller sees this message as an assault on my self-esteem, then he is rejecting God's plan and, like Adam and Eve in the garden, like Satan, he is trying to usurp the authority of God.

Schuller's church, while perhaps the most visible, is certainly not the only Christian organization where self-esteem is actively taught. I have seen books on building self-esteem used as material for adult Bible study classes in conservative, evangelical Baptist churches. Self-esteem is everywhere.

ORIGIN OF THE LIE

Where does our culture's preoccupation with self-esteem come from? Apart from the obvious answer that it is Satan's latest assault on the relationship between God and man, our interest in self-esteem can be seen as a logical outgrowth of the shift in thinking that began in the Renaissance and led eventually to post-Christian modernism and on to postmodernism. Francis Schaeffer describes some of this shift in *Escape from Reason*.[12]

According to Schaeffer, pre-Renaissance people thought in forms that were essentially Byzantine—heavenly things were all important, and nature was largely ignored. During the thirteenth century, however, people became more interested in nature for its own sake. While this shift in thinking was valuable in that it recognized nature's importance as a creation of God, it paved the way for a separation of man and his world into what eventually came to be seen as nonrational things, such as faith in God and optimism, and rational things, such as pessimism and secular humanism. Schaeffer called the irrational elements the "upper story" and the rational elements the "lower story." Today's assertion by many theologians that Christianity (or any other belief in God, for that matter) cannot be defended through logic, that it requires a "leap of faith" (ostensibly from the rational lower story to the irrational upper story), bears witness to the accuracy of Schaeffer's assessment of modern thinking.

Because the rational plane of modern thinking could admit only of a material reality, the universe came to be seen as no more than a machine. Any other view was considered irrational. Man was reduced to a mere cog in a cosmic apparatus, a pawn of forces beyond his control. In *Death in the City*, Francis Schaeffer summarized this plight of modern people:

> Increasingly educated, twentieth-century men tend to emphasize some sort of determinism. Usually it is one of two kinds: chemical determinism (such as the Marquis de Sade put forward and as Francis Crick maintains today) or psychological determinism (such as that emphasized by Freud and those who follow him). In the former, man is a pawn of chemical forces. In the latter, every decision that a man makes is already determined on the basis of what has occurred to him in the past. So whether it is chemical determinism or psychological determinism, man is no longer responsible for what he is or does, nor can he be active in making significant history. Man is no more than part of a cosmic machine.[13]

Schaeffer was concerned with the post-Christian, modern person of his day. He did not live long enough to see the cosmic machine of modernism give way to the random chance of postmodernism. In the postmodern view of reality, men and women are not even cogs in a cosmic machine, their actions pre-determined—because there is no machine. A machine at least implies order and purposeful activity. Now the machine is gone, and men and women are random accidents whose lives have no purpose. The belief in an ordered universe has been pushed into the irrational upper story along with the belief in God. It is small wonder that people today are desperate for self-esteem, for a feeling that they are important, that their lives have value and meaning.

Another reason for our culture's attraction to the lie of self-esteem is its utter plausibility. And it does contain a grain of truth.

After all, a healthy regard for the self is not inherently evil. Self-esteem is a creation of God and, like all of God's creations, it is good. As a trained zoologist, I see this instinct for self-love as part of our God-given survival mechanism. If we didn't care about ourselves at all, we wouldn't be as likely to defend ourselves or our young against danger. But our culture's preoccupation with self-esteem has perverted a good into an evil.

This distortion of self-esteem's importance has led to a seemingly endless proliferation of books on the subject. These books represent the latest installment in our attempt to find something to replace the God we have safely disposed of by pushing Him into Francis Schaeffer's irrational upper story. These books follow a long tradition of God-denying work, perhaps the most notable in this century being the writings of Freud and Frankl.

Both Freud and Frankl looked for a unifying theory to explain all human behavior, much the way Einstein looked for a unifying field theory to explain the physical universe. For Freud, that unifying theory became the drive for sex. For Frankl, it was the search for meaning. Both of these drives—sex and meaning—are important. And, like all aspects of God's creation, they are inherently good. But in and of themselves, they are insufficient to explain many human actions. And by focusing on them as the basis for all behavior, Freud and Frankl have distorted them and given them an importance they do not deserve.

Imagine what would happen if someone proposed a theory (and popularized it with a best-selling book) saying that the need to eat was the basic driving force that motivates all human behavior. Now you could actually make a pretty good case for this position. After all, food is the first means whereby we learn to trust another person, and it is an important aspect of our socialization. Ancient hospitality laws involve eating, and seldom do social functions take place without refreshments. Historically, food has been involved in territorial wars. Famines have led to mass migrations and cultural shifts. Even today food is used as a political weapon.

Nevertheless, by insisting that eating is our greatest desire and most basic need, this premise takes something that God has given us for our survival and our pleasure and exaggerates its importance all out of proportion. Pursued to its logical conclusion, this focus on food would make the sin of gluttony into a virtue. If eating is our basic human birthright and need, then we should all eat as much food as possible, hoard food, collect recipes, join dinner groups, focus all our attention on food. By fulfilling our basic human need, we can then achieve happiness and success.

The same sort of thing is happening with self-esteem. The self-esteem writers are telling us that the desire for self-love is a basic human birthright and a need that drives all our behaviors. Robert Schuller, who has elevated the search for self-love to a spiritual plane, asserts that self-love is our deepest desire; it is that around which our soul revolves.[14] In other words, what we need, what we desire, what motivates us, and what fulfills us is self-love.

Yes, it is necessary to have a certain healthy regard for one's self. Like eating, and like sex and the search for meaning, self-esteem enhances our survival chances and gives us pleasure. But the search for self-esteem is not the reason for our existence. Spending all of our time and energy trying to understand the causes of low self-esteem and enhancing our self-esteem has made the sin of self-centeredness into a virtue in our culture.

CONSEQUENCES OF THE LIE

Loss of legitimate shame and guilt

One of my favorite Doonesbury comic strips shows a young, obviously successful professional couple interviewing the pastor of Trudeau's fictional Little Church of Walden. When the pastor admits to using the occasional "disincentive" to keep his parishioners in line, the couple decides to look elsewhere, saying that they want a supportive church that will make them feel good about themselves.

One of the most obvious consequences of the lie of self-esteem is the loss of legitimate shame and guilt. Like the couple in Doonesbury, we all want to feel good about ourselves. Guilt makes us uncomfortable. It threatens our self-image, so we deny its validity. Nowhere have I seen this more blatantly illustrated than in the business video, *Building Self-Esteem: Realities of Human Behavior.* According to this video, we are never to blame for what we do, because our actions result from our prevailing awareness, over which we have no control. Though the video admits that we cannot escape responsibility for our actions, it asserts that we are not to blame for them. Therefore, we should never feel guilty. Blame and guilt block genuine self-love, the video's narrator says.[15]

This contention that shame should be avoided because it destroys self-esteem can be found in the work of religious as well as secular writers. Robert Schuller often links shame to a loss of self-esteem. In *Self-Esteem: The New Reformation*, Schuller writes that Christ encountered hell during His death on the cross because He experienced the loss of human pride. Schuller believes that a person without self-esteem is in hell.[16]

Lewis B. Smedes, Professor of Integrative Studies in the Graduate School at Fuller Theological Seminary, writes that shame makes us feel unworthy, and he denounces authority figures, including schools, churches, and parents, for shaming us. Even God comes under Smedes's indictment in his rather fanciful retelling of the Cain and Abel story. According to Smedes, God condemned Cain to shame, making him suffer a fate worse than death.[17] For some reason, Smedes chooses to ignore the fact that Cain's murder of his brother was not his first crime. It was only one in a series of sins that began with his offhand, impious offering to God. Impiety was followed by anger, jealousy, murder, and deception.

When Cain begs God to protect him from people who would

kill him for his crime, he is concerned about no one but himself. At no time does Cain express remorse, nor does he exhibit any of the guilt or shame that Smedes seems to blame God for imposing on him. God's act was one of unbelievable restraint and compassion. Many people today believe that a murderer should be executed. Not only did God not execute Cain, but He protected him from others who would do so, even threatening vengeance seven times over on anyone who harmed Cain. Where is the shame in this? And how can Smedes blame God for shaming Cain, when Cain clearly felt no shame himself?

And in a strange reinterpretation of the prodigal son story, Smedes writes that the father tells his faithful son that the prodigal is *worthy* to be his son.[18] Apparently, Smedes believes that the value of this story is that the father does not shame the prodigal son, but affirms his worth and bolsters his self-esteem. But this story is not about human worth. It is about God's limitless love, always available to those who repent, even to someone as obviously undeserving as the wastrel son. The prodigal was dead in sin and now is alive in repentance. Grace was given—but not because the prodigal son was worthy of it or because his self-esteem needed to be preserved. Indeed, the son readily admits, "I am no longer worthy to be called your son."[19] Grace is offered because the prodigal repents.

Even the secular world is beginning to recognize that the loss of legitimate shame and guilt is a serious problem. A recent issue of *Newsweek* carried several articles on shame, one of which reported on programs in which criminal offenders are expected to express remorse or are held up for public shame as part of their punishment. In another of these articles writer Kenneth L. Woodward warns that we are creating moral Frankenstein monsters when we excise guilt from our culture's psyche.[20]

But relieving us from our sense of sin is exactly what the self-esteem writers strive for. Schuller believes that scientific research will one day show that all inappropriate behavior results from our emotional need for self-love.[21] We are not sinful in any Biblical sense. We are only emotionally needy.

Schuller even goes so far as to identify original sin as a lack of self-esteem. According to Schuller, because we are born outside of paradise, we suffer from guilt-induced fear. Schuller tries to support his opinions by referring to the work of child psychologist Erik Erikson, who has suggested that we are all born fearful and nontrusting. Schuller interprets this theory to mean that we are born lacking in self-love or self-esteem. Schuller calls this view a scientific doctrine of original sin.[22] Scientific? Erikson's idea about the self-esteem or lack thereof in newborn infants is a theory, not scientific fact. Furthermore, Erikson's theories represent attempts to explain infant behavior; they have nothing to say about original sin.

Shifting responsibility

Former San Diego Mayor Roger Hedgecock has observed that nowadays no one acknowledges personal responsibility for his actions. We blame everything on nature or nurture, not on ourselves.[23]

Closely akin to the loss of legitimate shame and guilt that results from a distorted focus on self-esteem is the human penchant for shifting responsibility for one's actions to someone or something else. This shifting of responsibility is as old as Adam and Eve. When confronted with his disobedience, Adam blames the woman for giving him the apple. And, in a bold stroke of genius that would set the tone for generations of excuses, Adam also blames God for giving him the woman. (After all, Adam never asked for a partner. It was God's idea.) Not to be left holding the bag, Eve blames the serpent for deceiving her.

What I find particularly interesting about this story is that the serpent blames no one. Perhaps by this point, God had already struck the serpent dumb. Or perhaps Satan had already left the body of the serpent, seeing which way the wind was blowing. Or maybe Satan, in the form of the serpent, was proud of his accomplishment and quite eager to take full credit. Judging from his attacks on Job, Satan has no trouble standing before God as the accuser and tormenter of men. It is not a role he is ashamed of if, indeed, Satan is capable of shame, which seems unlikely. The serpent's role in this story also puzzles me in that if the serpent were only an unwitting host of Satan, why were the serpent and its descendants cursed? It would seem that the participation in evil is, for all creatures, perhaps for all creation, not just humankind, a voluntary action over which we can exercise choice and for which we must be held accountable. Much as we would like to believe otherwise, shifting responsibility is not really possible.

Death of critical thought

In a much-quoted study that compared middle school students from six different countries, including the United States, researchers learned that while American children ranked a dismal last in mathematics, they generally rated their math ability high. "Despite their poor overall performance . . . two-thirds of U.S. thirteen-year-olds felt that 'they are good at mathematics'; only 23 percent of their Korean counterparts shared that attitude."[24] (Korean students, by the way, scored first in math.) Commenting on this study, a public education critic and founder of the Christian Logos School in Moscow, Idaho, has written, "When it comes to maintaining a high self-image, we can take on the world."[25]

Clearly, high self-esteem does nothing to ensure that we think critically about ourselves or the world we live in, a world God expects us to engage on an intellectual level. In fact, the emphasis of self-esteem literature on our worthiness, our uniqueness, our basic goodness, and our lovability despite or sometimes even because of our flaws demands that at times we totally abandon critical thought. Like the writings of other inspirational cults, self-esteem literature displays "a withdrawal from reality, a repudiation of all philosophies whose business is an engagement with real problems," according to historian Richard Hofstadter.[26]

Theologian Richard John Neuhaus argues that the position of self-esteem advocates, such as Norman Vincent Peale, is untenable because you cannot embrace the positive while ignoring the negative. To do so is to abandon rational thought. Neuhaus rightly points out that "we should dislike much about ourselves, because there is much about ourselves that is not only profoundly dislikable but odious."[27] Christian psychologist Alan Loy McGinnis agrees, warning that it is irrational to tell people to love that which should not be loved.[28] No one is wonderful at all times and in every way.

The apparent surrender of any attempt to teach children to think critically about themselves, about the world around them, and about their place in society is amply illustrated in a manual written for teaching self-esteem in the classroom. In one of the exercises suggested by the authors, the children are instructed to look inside a box where, they are told, they will see the most important person in the world. As you would expect, inside the box is a mirror, and each child sees himself. But no one (certainly not the authors of this self-esteem tract) bothers to question the rationality of believing that you are the most important person in the world. Does it really make sense to teach an entire classroom of children that each one is the most important person? Furthermore, does believing the unbelievable really create self-esteem?

In his work on the "inner child" and self-esteem, psychologist Bruce Davis has clearly delivered the corpse of critical thought to the morgue. Davis insists that physical ailments are a result of the inner child needing attention. Apparently, his idea is that when we don't love ourselves enough, our bodies rebel by making us ill. According to Davis, a sore knee is really my inner child telling me he feels crippled. Davis also believes that headaches are the child banging for attention, and backaches are the child feeling that the whole world is on his back.[29] It is this abandonment of critical thought and scientific inquiry that once convinced people that ulcers result from bottled-up emotions and schizophrenia and autism from early childhood trauma. We now know that ulcers are caused by bacteria and aggravated by aspirin; schizophrenia and autism are genetic defects in brain neurochemistry.

The divorce of critical thought from the self-esteem movement can be seen clearly in the popular press. A recent issue of a women's magazine that revealed the "secrets" of self-esteem and told readers not to be too hard on themselves also carried articles on losing weight, trimming inches off bulging hips, wearing make-up to look better, getting a more flattering haircut, and dealing with disappointing children. Obviously, the magazine does not expect its readers to really think. If they did, they would see the inconsistency in the advice being given.

Roy F. Baumeister, liberal arts professor at Case Western Reserve University, explains this death of critical thought as part of our culture's need to escape the tremendous burden of the self. The unremitting pressure to love and satisfy ourselves, central to self-esteem programs, can become intolerable, according to Baumeister. He maintains that we seek escape by focusing our attention only on the present and on our physical bodies, and by rejecting meaningful thought.[30]

It is significant that self-esteem writer David Burns, who pioneered and tested his self-esteem program at the Presbyterian Medical Center in Philadelphia, believes that once you learn unconditional self-esteem, you can discard the whole notion entirely and move on to a higher level of functioning. What is that higher level? A kind of Buddhist renunciation of the self. According to Burns, you gain the world when you discover that you are nothing.[31] This is the plight of postmodern men and women living in a culture that tells them on the one hand to love themselves and on the other hand that they are nothing. To embrace both is to deny all attempts at critical discourse. We are left with only Francis Schaeffer's irrational upper story. There is no lower story anymore. Nothing is rational.

Changing places with God

In the logic of self-esteem, man does not exist, as the Westminster Catechism asserts, "to glorify God and to enjoy Him forever." Rather, God exists to affirm man and make him feel good about himself. God is our enabler, our giver of self-esteem. According to psychiatrist Michael P. Nichols, religion satisfies unconscious needs and can promote self-respect.[32] Christian writer Earl Wilson identifies God as our source of self-acceptance.[33] And Rabbi Kushner teaches that a major goal of religion is to help us like ourselves.[34] Perhaps a new self-esteem catechism might claim that man exists to be glorified by God and affirmed by Him forever.

Clearly, Robert Schuller believes strongly in this role reversal. Sin, for example, is anything that robs us of self-esteem. Schuller finds the definition of sin as rebellion against God shallow and insulting to people. And Schuller calls for a new reformation in which we focus on the human right to self-esteem. He notes that classical theology is wrong when it insists on a God-centered, not a man-centered, theology. (Apparently, Schuller does not know what the word *theology* means.) Ostensibly writing to Christians, Schuller recommends that we use human beings as the theological launching point. And Schuller titles the last chapter of his book on the new reformation, "Self-Esteem: The Universal Hope." Our hope is not God, not Christ, not the cross, not even the Christian church, but self-esteem. Here is a new religion that has given up all pretense of worshiping God. Man is the focus of man's devotion. God is important only in what He can do for us.[35]

Of course, some self-esteem writers simply ignore God's role in our lives altogether. For these writers, the self is sufficient unto itself. Therefore, achieving self-esteem becomes our highest and most fulfilling calling. Feel-good author and lecturer Leo Buscaglia tells us that we alone create and define our own happiness.[36] Bruce Davis's road to self-esteem includes releasing the inner child as one chooses one's own way, free of external pressures. But this inner child has disturbing pantheistic elements. Davis tells us that he and the world are one; both share his experience.[37] These writers, the Shirley MacLaines who have the chutzpah to openly declare, "I am God," do not merely have man reverse roles with God; man usurps both roles.

WHAT THE BIBLE SAYS ABOUT SELF-ESTEEM

A few years back, a pop music superstar hit the top of the charts with a song about the greatest love of all. The love she sang about was not the love of a parent for a child, the love of one spouse for another, the love of a martyr for his cause, the love of a patriot for his country, not even, sadly, the love of man for God. No, the object of love in that song was the self. The greatest love of all is the love I have for myself. This is the love, and the attitude about love, that the self-esteem proponents are so determined to inculcate in our children in the public schools and in our cultural thinking through the mass media.

As Christians, we have a responsibility to resist popular pressure and look instead to Scripture for answers. So just what does the Bible say about esteem, about love, and about how we are supposed to think of ourselves?

The Bible has a great deal to say about love; *NIV Nave's Topical Bible* includes six pages on the subject. (And that's in very small print!) Biblical passages on love describe the quality of love, the expression of love, the types of love, the results of love, the value of love, examples of love, commandments about love, the love of God, and the love of Jesus. But in not one single instance does the Bible recommend, commend, or command self-love or self-esteem.

The closest we get to any sort of self-love advice is the commandment to love others as we love ourselves, a commandment that appears in both the Old and New Testaments.[38] Unfortunately, this commandment has been distorted by both secular and religious writers to be a commandment for self-love, the implication being that we cannot really love others unless and until we learn to love ourselves. Leo Buscaglia, Bruce Davis, and Shirley MacLaine are all typical of self-esteem writers in insisting that we must learn to love ourselves before we can truly love and accept other people. These writers all attempt to raise selfishness to a spiritual level. But this is not what the Bible says.

The commandment that I love others as I love myself gives me an example to follow in my treatment of other people. It is a commandment of action, of duty, not one of feelings, and it makes the reasonable assumption that my actions toward myself show natural self-regard. I keep my body clean, I feed it, I clothe it, and I provide it with shelter. I entertain my mind with books, music, television, movies, visits with friends and relatives. I see a dentist every six months to keep my teeth healthy. I go to a doctor when I am ill. (Okay, I should probably go for regular check-ups, but I'm not overly fond of medical procedures.) Even people who report feelings of very low self-esteem do the same sort of things, taking remarkably good care of themselves. Actually, by focusing so much attention on themselves and their self-esteem problem, these people demonstrate quite unequivocally the interest they have in themselves. If we can do this much for ourselves, God expects us to do no less for other people.

More than that, the Bible tells us we should actually regard others above ourselves. Paul makes this responsibility clear in his letter to the Romans. "Be devoted to one another in brotherly love. Honor one another above yourselves."[39] In Philippians, Paul advises us, "Do nothing out of selfish ambition or vain conceit, but in humility consider others better than yourselves."[40] And Jesus did not tell us, as the pop song does, that the greatest love of all is that which we show ourselves. On the contrary, He taught, "Greater love has no one than this, that he lay down his life for his friends."[41]

What a contrast Jesus' teachings are to the work of self-esteem expert Nathaniel Branden, who insists that the moral ideal of self-sacrifice should be abandoned.[42] Relationships should be based on a mutual exchange of values, according to Branden, as if we can weigh such intangibles as love and respect and dignity on a grocer's scales. But then Brandon is openly hostile to religion, claiming that religious orthodoxy is opposed to the human exercise of conscious living and that God is the enemy of man and his right to self-esteem.

If the Bible is clear about how and who we are to love, it is also clear about how we are to think of ourselves—humbly. The Bible has almost as many references to humility and its opposite, pride, as to love. The Israelites were commanded to remember that they had been mere slaves in Egypt, and the people of God were always warned not to exalt themselves.[43] Jesus taught that those who humbled themselves would be exalted in heaven.[44] And Paul made it clear that he never boasted (and Paul had more right than most of us to feel quite pleased with himself) save in the cross of Jesus Christ.[45] Paul repeatedly warned others to live humbly and avoid pride and conceit.[46] Likewise, James recommended humility.[47] The greatest giants of both the Old and New Testaments are remembered for their humility. Abraham, made the father of two great nations, admitted that he was "nothing but dust and ashes."[48] Jacob expressed his unworthiness,[49] as did Moses[50] and David.[51] And in one of my favorite psalms, David marvels that God would be interested in a creature as insignificant as man.[52]

The Bible tells us to consider ourselves with humility, to put others first, and to love other people with the same care and devotion we naturally lavish on ourselves. What of esteem? According to the Bible, the only esteem worth striving for is the esteem of God. Throughout Scripture, the righteous seek God's esteem, while the foolish and the wicked worry about the esteem of men.

And how do we receive God's esteem? Certainly not by being a man or woman created in the image of God or even being loved by God. For these "accomplishments," God offers us salvation. Daniel received God's esteem. How? By living righteously, by praying, fasting, working for the reconciliation of God with the Israelites, by keeping God's laws. Abel received God's favor because of his offering. Throughout the Old Testament we read that God looks with favor on those who obey Him; He esteems those who are humble and contrite in spirit.[53]

The wonder of human existence, as taught to us in the Bible, is not that we are worthy or deserving or lovable. It is not that we can fulfill ourselves or anyone else. The wonder is that God is always available to make us worthy and deserving and lovable by filling us with Himself. The wonder is that Completeness, that Self-Sufficiency, that Perfection, that Infinity, that God would concern Himself with us. Why should I waste my time gnawing on the dry bread of my own love for myself when I can feast on the banquet of God's love for me?

9

Lie Six:
I Need to Learn
Positive Self-Talk

For the last chapter in this section, I have saved what I believe may be the most insidious lie of the self-help movement because of its plausibility. This lie feeds on the American obsession with selfhood, and it is foremost in all modern self-help programs, be they secular or religious. That lie is the notion that I need to learn and actively practice positive self-talk.

It is probably unnecessary to define self-talk, positive or otherwise, in our talk-saturated culture. But just in case there are a few people who are still unfamiliar with the concept, here goes. Self-talk is what you say when you talk to yourself. (With me so far?) It exists, according to at least one "expert," at various levels.[1] The lowest and most damaging level is *negative* self-talk. You might use it when you trip over something and call yourself clumsy or when you get passed over for promotion and tell yourself that you're never going to amount to anything. A higher level of self-talk involves *positive* affirmations about the self, such as, "I'm really good at motivating people to get things done."

Proponents of positive self-talk insist that most of us talk to ourselves most of the time in fairly negative ways. This negative self-talk supposedly manifests itself in negative behaviors—the old self-fulfilling prophecy idea. Positive self-talk advocates also tell us we can learn to use positive self-talk—what really amounts to positive affirmations about the self—and, thus, permanently change our behavior for the better. This positive self-talk, they say, is the real key to success, to recovery, to self-esteem—all the wonderful goals of the self-help movement. Positive self-talk, the experts insist, is the critical ingredient without which no self-improvement program will produce lasting results.

Positive self-talk is effective, we are told, because the unconscious mind works like a computer; it believes anything you tell it, and it acts on that belief. Thus, if you tell yourself that you are clumsy, your unconscious mind will believe you and will see to it that you trip and stumble. Similarly, if you tell yourself that you are a brilliant organizer, your unconscious mind will set about to organize your life.

The positive self-talk assertion relies on two basic assumptions that, for reasons unclear to me, are seldom challenged. The first is that we all talk to ourselves in very negative ways most of the time. Our natural self-talk is supposedly damaging and hostile to the self. Self-talk proponents often cite "evidence" of the numbers of times we bombard ourselves with negative messages. According to their reasoning, we internalize these messages, thereby sabotaging our effectiveness or our belief in our abilities. Negative self-talk supposedly wreaks havoc in our lives, causing chaos and self-doubt, crippling our chances for happiness and success.

Positive self-talk advocates, however, fail to cite any controlled research studies that would support their assertions, choosing to rely on anecdotal evidence. Now I admit that such data may exist. But without the relevant research reports in hand, I can say nothing about methodology, data collection, statistical analyses, or the researchers' conclusions.

I have, however, read reports that paint a very different picture. For example, a study of math and science performance and self-rated competence showed that American children, despite their dismal objective performance on math and science tests, believed themselves to be good at math.[2] Obviously, their self-talk must be rather positive. Social psychologist David G. Myers reports that annual surveys by the National Opinion Research Center at the University of Chicago reveal that the vast majority of Americans rate themselves as satisfied with life. Fewer than 10 percent claim to being more dissatisfied than satisfied.[3] And in a cross-national survey of personal satisfaction, Americans showed up on the high end of the scale, reporting levels of satisfaction well above the French, Japanese, Italians, Spanish, Greeks, Germans, and Austrians.[4] With so much good feeling abroad in America, can we really be filling our minds with the constant negativity that self-talk experts say we are?

The second assumption made by self-talk proponents is far more serious because it speaks to our modern notion of what it means to be human, and it hints at the workings of very dark forces in our collective consciousness. That is the assumption that the human mind works like a computer. While this assumption sounds fairly innocuous, what it really says is that mankind is a device, a thing. Furthermore, it maintains that the human brain processes discrete bits of information according to fixed rules and that it can be manipulated by forces it fails to recognize and over which it has no control.

This mechanistic view of human life is not new. We see echoes of it in the writings of behavioral psychologists and their "black box" notions of human activity. And we have been warned about it by poets and philosophers down through the ages. Madeleine L'Engle with her portrayal of Camazotz in *A Wrinkle in Time,* C. S. Lewis with his disembodied head in the scientific community of Belbury in *That Hideous Strength*, George Orwell with his totalitarian regime in *1984* are only a few of the writers who tell us how freedom is lost, how creativity is stifled, how society stagnates when men and women are viewed as machines to be manipulated without their knowledge or consent.

Not only are there dangerous consequences in thinking of the human mind as a computer (after all, computers can be programmed), but the analogy is feeble and shows that the writers who make it really understand very little about either human or computer intelligence. Let me make it clear that I have no intention of explaining either computers or brains in any exhaustive way. (In any event, I'm not qualified to do so. If you want a thorough critique of this whole mind/computer issue, I invite you to read *What Computers Still Can't Do: A Critique of Artificial Reason* by MIT Professor Hubert L. Dreyfus.) With that caveat firmly in mind, here are the basic problems with the computer/brain analogy.[5]

1. On a purely physical level, there is no evidence that computers and human brains work in the same way. Computers operate digitally with a series of on/off switches. The human brain may contain neurons that fire in an all or none fashion, but neurobiologists have found that these firings have less to do with individual, discrete events, as in computers, than with global functioning.

2. Computers process information one bit at a time. There is no empirical evidence to suggest that either the human brain or its psychological correlate, the human mind, works in this way, processing one piece of information, completing one step in a program, and then moving on to the next. The convolutions of one's own reasoning, the serendipity of discovery, the quantum leaps in understanding that all humans make must certainly belie that notion on a merely practical, experiential level.

3. Computers follow the rules of their programs. Again there is no evidence to suggest that human beings think via a system of rules or programs. The view that human thinking can be reduced to data processing assumes that the processor (you or me) must play no essential role in thinking. If this were true, then human beings would not vary so widely in their perception, interpretation, analysis, and use of the same information. This assumption, and that which posits thinking as a sequential operation performed on discrete bits of information, reduces human beings to stimulus-response mechanisms.

4. Computers have no body. The human body, with its sensory capacity, its endocrine system, its emotions, its kinesthetic memory, its gender, even its aches and pains, contributes to human intelligence and thinking. When I have a headache, I can barely follow the plot of a simple mystery story. When I am in love, I interpret the neutral expressions of the people around me as mirrors of my own joy. When I am hungry, I notice food imagery in works of art. Computers have no such mind-body communication and interaction.

The assertion that the human brain operates like a computer is just one more attempt, like that of C. S. Lewis's evil Belbury, to separate man's mind from his body. It denies or at least ignores the role of the body, of man's physical presence, in intelligence. Clearly God must care a lot about matter; He created so much of it. There is no reason to assume that the body exists merely to house the mind or soul. Why not just create disembodied spirits? It seems clear that God intended the human body to function with the brain in creating human intellect.

All of these rather abstruse arguments aside, the self-talk assertion that the human brain works like a computer and that we can change our behavior by reprogramming our thoughts breaks down when one looks at it sensibly. A computer does not use the information it is given to change itself in any way. I cannot, by telling my computer daily that it is capable of storing as much information as I need, encourage it to expand its memory capacity. My computer can never be more or less than it was engineered to be. The self-talk people would have us believe that by telling ourselves positive things, we will become those things, because the unconscious mind works like a computer. What nonsense.

JOURNALING

An outgrowth of the self-talk movement is the written version known as journaling. Keeping a journal is recommended by positive self-talk experts who see journaling as a way to uncover one's *true* feelings. Once you know what your feelings are, you can work to change negative feelings by feeding yourself positive information. Other self-help experts, including religious writers such as Charles Swindoll, recommend journaling as a way to track progress in whatever your endeavor may be—spiritual growth or a healthier diet or a more affable temperament.

The evangelical members of Churches Alive International advocate journaling because they believe that the most important aspect of Bible study is personal experience.[6] One journaling trainer says that the journal process helps us reconstruct our lives by pulling us along our life process.[7] But do we really need to be drawn along our life process? Won't life proceed whether we will have it or no? The same journaling expert also asserts that the journal functions to establish a dialogue between our inner self and our external existence.[8] Again the point of journaling here seems to be self-talk. The whole concept reminds me of nothing so much as a manual for autoeroticism. But dialogues, like sex, are meant to include another person.

What much of today's journaling, like self-talk, is really about is self-centeredness and self-indulgence. After his conversion, C. S. Lewis was quick to recognize this truth. In *Surprised by Joy*, he admits, ". . . one of the first results of my Theistic conversion was a marked decrease in the fussy attentiveness which I had so long paid to the progress of my own opinions and the states of my own mind. . . . If Theism has done nothing else for me, I should still be thankful that it cured me of the time-wasting and foolish practice of keeping a diary."[9] Even before he became a Christian, while still a theist, C. S. Lewis recognized the nonsense of a practice designed only to keep our attention focused on ourselves.

Any self-focus, even if the reason seems to be meritorious, such as charting our progress in self-denial or spiritual awareness, always interferes with Christian discipleship. "To deny oneself is to be aware only of Christ and no more of self," Dietrich Bonhoeffer tells us.[10] What is self-talk, what is most journaling, but a way of remaining always and particularly aware of the self?

Peter found out firsthand what happens when you take your eyes off Christ and think about what you are doing. You sink.

ORIGIN OF THE LIE

The lie of self-talk has its roots in the "mind power" notions of the nineteenth century. Pioneered by, among others, Phineas Parkhurst Quimby, a clockmaker who traded cogs for psychic healing, this movement gave birth to Christian Science. It preached that man is divine, with infinite possibilities.[11] Mind power persists today in New Age doctrines teaching that we are all God and co-masters of the cosmos. We only need to awaken or get in touch with our god inside to have the abundant life.

It is easy for Christians to dismiss reincarnated crystal freaks with a few sarcastic jokes. But what about the mind power movement that is firmly entrenched in American Protestantism? What do we say to the millions of people who still read Norman Vincent Peale and are convinced of the power of positive thinking? Or what of the millions who follow Robert Schuller and his possibility thinking? Positive self-talk merely extends positive thinking by creating a specific self-affirming monologue that we are encouraged to present to ourselves on a daily basis. These speeches to ourselves are supposed to create the positive programming that allows our brains to direct our bodies to live successfully. With our words, we create our own reality.

Many ostensibly Christian mind power advocates base their assertions on the first half of one single verse of Scripture— Proverbs 23:7. The King James version of this half verse reads, "For as he thinketh in his heart, so is he." Self-talk and positive thinking proponents interpret this sentence to mean that human beings become the living result of what they think. As a popular motivational phrase puts it, "What you think about, you bring about."

But a close study of this section of Scripture reveals a very different interpretation. This sentence is part of a section of Proverbs containing sayings "to encourage faith in God, to admonish, and to instruct the one seeking wisdom."[12] In particular, chapter 23 includes advice on table etiquette and the folly of amassing wealth. Verses 6-8 in the *New International Version* read: "Do not eat the food of a stingy man, do not crave his delicacies; for he is the kind of man who is always thinking about the cost. 'Eat and drink,' he says to you, but his heart is not with you. You will vomit up the little you have eaten and will have wasted your compliments."

The *Evangelical Commentary on the Bible* says of these verses: "The wise man should not dine with a miserly (Heb. evil eye) person, nor desire to do so, because though outwardly pleasant, he is actually grudging the guest his food. Should this unfortunate situation occur, it will sicken the guest."[13]

Where do we find any hint that the writer of Proverbs is telling us that the thoughts of man create his behavior? The behavior of the miserly host is not a reflection of the thoughts of his heart, which begrudge the food he gives to his guest, but an attempt to cover them up. Looking at this passage of the Bible provides us with a perfect illustration of one of the first rules of Bible study— never take a verse out of context.

Ultimately, the lie of positive self-talk can be traced to man's desire to usurp God's role. God called forth the universe with His Word. Now man claims the power to create himself with his own words. More than that, the self-talk proponents believe we can even create the cosmos with our words, because reality is a result of our perception, they say. Change the words, change the belief, change the perception, change the reality. We can remake the universe to suit ourselves simply by talking.

CONSEQUENCES OF THE LIE

Loss of objectivity

Objectivity is the state of external or material reality. When we talk about objective information, we are talking about something that exists apart from personal prejudice or bias; something that will yield the same measurement, no matter who is doing the measuring; something that is based on observable phenomena. Something that has objective reality can be said to actually exist. Objectivity is the opposite of relativity.

Self-talk proponents operate on the assumption that there is no objective truth or reality. Truth is whatever we program ourselves to believe. If we don't like a particular "truth," such as the truth that we have two left feet, for example, we can simply deny that unacceptable reality and tell ourselves repeatedly that we have the grace of Ginger Rogers or Fred Astaire. According to the self-talk notion, if we regularly tell ourselves with conviction, "I am as graceful as Ginger Rogers. I dance through my day with beauty in every step," we will alter reality, creating a new truth in which we are indeed very graceful.

But the relativism of self-talk does not create truth. No matter how much I convince myself of that which is not true, my belief cannot make it true. "Even though we are often convinced of our own beliefs because we somehow feel them strongly, those feelings can hardly be a reliable guide for truth. Truth has to be assessed in some other way," explains Christian apologist Winfried Corduan.[14] That other way includes feedback from a source outside myself. Despite the insistence of self-talk proponents that we listen only to our own positive self-talk and ignore negative input or contradictory statements from other people, the most accurate way to assess ourselves is through the objective scrutiny of someone with no personal axe to grind or through looking into the mirror of God's Word. (I am not, of course, suggesting that the feedback from a rival or an enemy or a lover will be necessarily objective simply because it originates outside the self.)

The limitation of self-talk can be seen clearly in the simple pleasure we all naturally feel when someone else recognizes our accomplishments. Human beings do not exist in isolation. We are creatures of community. This community not only serves for our mutual protection and well-being, but it keeps us in touch with objective reality.

When one embraces self-talk to the exclusion of objective reality, the descent into fantasy can never be far behind. But so determined are the mind power advocates to hang on to their beliefs that they imbue their gibberish with a kind of spurious science by trying to prove that reality is only a matter of personal sensory experience. One of the most striking examples appears in *The Wizdom Within: On Daydreams, Realities and Revelations.* In a chapter called "The Reality Fantasy," authors Irving Oyle and Susan Jean state that reality is simply a matter of personal choice.[15] These authors also insist that we can change reality by changing belief, because reality is nothing more than personal perception, which is based on belief.[16]

What Oyle and Jean, and many other writers like them, are saying is that objective reality doesn't exist. All we have is the "reality" of our own minds, our own beliefs, our own perceptions. But since these, as the authors admit themselves, are constantly changing, reality is constantly changing. We are Alice trapped in Wonderland with no objective frame of reference or route of escape. We are caged in a fantasy universe of our own making.

Why is this argument so dangerous? Because without objective reality, human civilization disappears. There can, for example, be no science. Scientific investigation is built firmly on the belief that an objectively real universe exists, that it is the same for all people, and that it behaves in predictable ways. And without objective reality, there can be no God. God is the author of reality. He exists outside of creation. He has set in motion a universe that follows predictable laws, a universe that is verifiable, that is quantifiable, and that is constant for all people in all times. We may understand only a small part of that reality, but our understanding does not change the reality. Our understanding of God does not change His nature. But by denying this objective reality, we deny God.

Human manipulation

The self-talk assertion that the human brain is like a computer and that it can be programmed reduces mankind to a kind of living machine. Is this idea serious? Of course it is. Because, like all ideas, it has consequences. One of those consequences is the use of virtual reality (VR) as a means for shaping and controlling human behavior. This may sound like science fiction, but the mind power gurus Irving Oyle and Susan Jean are serious when they insist that VR is just as real as the reality we ordinarily live in, because it can be shared by other people who "plug in" with us. More than that, Oyle and Jean believe that VR is better because it can be programmed. In their view of the future VR world, the human brain will become a single unit in a global, interconnected VR network. We will be able to create and share any reality we wish.[17]

This vision is not the invention of a science-fiction writer or a prophet of doom. It is the prediction, the happy expectation, of psychotherapists who see human beings as characters in a computer-generated fantasy world. This is the ultimate in mind control because it provides the ability to manipulate people by giving them what they most want—a pleasurable reality. Never mind that the reality is an electronic fantasy. People who plug in will experience it as if it were real.

Oyle and Jean believe that if we can choose our own reality, we will naturally choose one that makes life more pleasant.[18] But what they fail to acknowledge is that reality on a computer level is not reality. Eventually we all have to unplug. What will we do with the reality we find outside our programmed minds? And if we choose to remain plugged in, what will happen to civilization, to the arts and sciences, to learning?

Gnosticism

Shad Helmstetter, one of the original proponents of self-talk, believes that the highest form of self-talk is the level of universal affirmation in which we acknowledge our oneness with God. At this level of self-talk, you might tell yourself that you and the universe are united into one perfect cosmic being that exists as a brilliant spark of the divine life and goodness.[19]

Helmstetter's highest level of self-talk is a modern expression of the very old religion, gnosticism. According to gnostic teaching, the soul is free of the created and fallen world. It is perfect and pre-existent with God. When a human being dies, his perfect soul returns to the divine plane from which it came. The corruptible is discarded as the perfect soul passes through ever higher spheres until it finally enters God and reasserts its divinity.[20]

The gnosticism of self-talk is part and parcel of what religious critic Harold Bloom calls the American religion. According to Bloom, Americans believe in a special contact with God that is unique to our view of ourselves. The self, as an American construct, is not a part of creation. It is as old as God. It exists with God. It is part of God.[21]

WHAT THE BIBLE SAYS ABOUT THE VOICE OF AUTHORITY

The characters of the Bible do a lot of talking and even, on occasion, some listening. The voices they listen to, either by command or choice, may be of God, rulers, judges, the righteous, and even the evil one. What we don't find in the Bible are people listening to themselves. Neither David, nor Daniel, nor Moses, nor Paul listened to their own self-talk. Not one of the Bible's great heroes or even its most desperate villains hearkened to his own voice. He didn't always listen to God, and he may have listened to foolish counselors, but he did not dialogue with himself. He did not tell himself what a great job he was doing ruling Palestine or driving away evil or keeping the law. Boasts in the Bible are intended for ears other than the boaster's, and they are always met with condemnation.

But all that aside, what we find most when we look for passages about speaking in the Bible is the voice of God. Sounding like the tumult of an army or thunder or the wings of angels, God's voice commands and receives attention. When you hear God's voice, you fall on your face.

Who hears God's voice? Certainly not the person whose ears are full of his own voice, the person who turns away to attend to other gods. No, those who hear God's voice are listening for it and expecting it. They are people who, according to Jesus, have ears to hear.[22] John tells us that Jesus said, "My sheep listen to my voice; I know them,"[23] and, "Everyone on the side of truth listens to me."[24] And what happens when you hear God and believe? The Holy Spirit comes.[25] The Holy Spirit of God, not a good feeling about the self or a sense of personal affirmation.

And when God talks, things happen. God spoke, and all of creation came into being. His words bring law, justice, righteousness, freedom, and wisdom. David tells us in one of his songs that we should listen to God, because he promises peace.[26] God speaks to make Himself known to us and to discipline us: "From heaven he made you hear his voice to discipline you."[27] Both Moses and Saul were granted the honor of hearing God. They listened and submitted themselves to God's discipline. As a result, murderers though they were, they became messengers of God, bringing God's deliverance, God's salvation to mankind.

And what about those negative words from other people that the self-talk experts are so afraid of? Well, the Bible tells us plainly that if the words come from wise men, we should listen. "It is better to heed a wise man's rebuke than to listen to the song of fools."[28]

The self-talk experts are right about one thing: we do have a choice about which voice we will listen to. Will that voice be our own, governed by our human failings and limitations, or will it be the voice of God? Will we follow in the steps of Paul and Moses, hearing and obeying, or will we fill our ears with the "song of fools" as we heed our own voices?

PART III

The Challenge for Christians

10

The Self-Help
Movement as a Religion

W hen something other than God becomes the focus of attention, it is tempting to label that thing as an idol and to describe the activity around it as a religion. We've heard this charge leveled so many times about so many things—money, sex, power, politics, psychology—that we tend to dismiss the argument as mere hyperbole, rather on the order of Jesus telling us to gouge out the eye that offends us. He was trying to make a point, warning us that sin needs to be dealt with drastically, not advocating self-mutilation. (After all, even a one-eyed or a blind man can have lustful thoughts.) In the same way, we assume that charges of a false religion are made to shake us out of our complacency, to warn us of the possible implications of our actions, to bring us to a state of repentance, and to return us to a proper focus on God. But we never suppose that the charge is meant literally.

I believe that the self-help movement in America today qualifies as a bona fide religion. In saying this, I am not exaggerating to make a point. Nor am I suggesting that its appearance as a religion was an accident or that its prime movers are unaware of the cult nature of the movement they have created. However, I will admit that many of its adherents (perhaps even most) are ignorant of the implications of their devotion to self-help. Self-help is, and has always been, as Richard Hofstadter observed more than thirty years ago, spiritual in nature.[1] Psychiatrist David Burns has similarly commented that self-esteem attitudes and beliefs share many features with traditional religion.[2]

Self-help does more than satisfy the broad and rather vague definition of religion as a way of life based on one's view of reality. Self-help also satisfies the more rigorous definition of a formal, communal religion in that it directs a sort of worship toward a specific faith object, and it displays the three necessary elements of a religion—creed, code, and cult.

CREED

Credo. I believe. Belief is the first and most important requirement of any religion. What must you do to be saved—by Jesus or Allah or Jehovah or a twelve-step program or self-esteem or success? You must believe. This is exactly what all self-help programs require of their disciples. Self-help writers insist that we must believe in their program before we can expect to see results. We are told that whatever the mind can conceive and believe, it can achieve. We are told that programming belief into the subconscious mind will produce the results we desire. Affirmation writers tell us that positive statements, made with belief, will become true. Whatever we want to have, whatever we want to be, belief is the first step. One self-help coach, determined that his clients not miss this point, actually tells them to write out a creed, a formal statement of what they believe about themselves. Faith in that creed, belief in that belief, he tells them, is the most important thing in their lives.[3]

But what are we to believe in? What is the object that inspires our statement of faith? In Christianity we profess faith in God the Father Almighty, in Jesus Christ His only Son, and in the Holy Ghost, who proceeds from the Father and the Son. In the religion of self-help, the object of worship is not the Triune God or any other god, for that matter, but the self. The theologians of this religion extol the self that is I AM, that is Abundance, that is Perfection, that is the god or goddess within. I am told to believe in myself, in my power of positive thinking, in my power of possibility thinking, in my success, in my greatness, in my human dignity and value, even in myself as the image of the divine. Robert Schuller delivers the most unequivocal version of this call to worship the self when he advocates a new theology centered on man.

CODE

The code of a religion is its system of laws and morals. It is the rules by which believers act out their creed. Judaism, for example, has more than 400 laws that the orthodox observer must abide by in order to be part of the faith community. (I once heard a rabbi say that everyone should obey the Ten Commandments, but only a Jew could be expected to follow all the other laws!)

Moral behavior—righteousness, if you will—can be a little trickier for Christians than for Jews, because Christianity is based not on law, but on grace. Salvation by grace can lead to all sorts of moral lapses, as anyone can see by reading Corinthians. And the belief that Christians are not bound by law continues to be used as an excuse for unrighteousness today. Nevertheless, Jesus made it clear that we are expected to act in ways that fulfill the commandment to love God and one another. And James emphasized that faith without works is dead.[4] Christianity's law is the rule of love and the claims of discipleship to Christ.

Self-help, too, has its code, its system for putting belief into practice. What does that code consist of? Simply all the strategies and tactics of self-improvement: goal-setting, prioritizing, time management, self-acceptance, positive visualization, positive self-talk, journaling, avoiding negative companions and influences, and values clarification—to name but a few. The practice of these laws, the faithful are told, will lead to the abundant life, rather in the way that the practice of righteousness earns someone stars in heaven. Of course, the self-help religion has the ostensible advantage of offering its treasures in a tangible way in the here and now.

CULT

The final element of formal religion—cult—encompasses the ritual of worship. Some common aspects of worship ritual are community gathering, group and individual prayers, the reading of sacred texts, the confession of sin, singing, the recitation of creeds, personal testimonies, instruction in the faith, and the practice of memorial rites. It does not take any great stretch of the imagination to discern these features in the practice of self-help.

The community of worship

Recovery groups typically display nearly all the aspects of formal worship. They gather as a group on a regular, usually weekly, basis. They read the purpose or mission statement of the group. Various members of the group stand up to "confess" that they are alcoholics or shopaholics or child abusers or codependents or overeaters or whatever. Other members tell how the group meetings are helping them become "whole," and a group leader gives a talk that usually includes both inspiration and practical information.

Other self-improvement programs may hold less frequent gatherings, but they generate more excitement. These are the self-help movement's version of revival meetings, and their function is to "convert" attenders to the program presented. Success, self-esteem, happiness, and human greatness movements typically operate their worship along these evangelistic lines. Here we see enthusiastic praise singing ("If you're happy and you know it, clap your hands!"), testimonies by individuals whose lives have been changed by the program being offered, and motivational and inspirational speakers. Often the audience is asked to repeat certain key phrases, telling each other, themselves, and the speaker how wonderful or full of abundance or happy or unlimited or successful they are—a kind of collective prayer of praise to the self. The price of admission to these seminars serves the role of a free-will collection in a Protestant church, although the typical large fee creates an impression of value in the attenders' minds.

The emphasis on community in self-help worship can also be seen in the work of organizations such as The Option Institute in Massachusetts and the Esalen Institute in California. They offer "retreats" for "seekers" who want to learn happiness or self-fulfillment. Participants gather to learn about and experience the midlife crisis as a time of spiritual change or the human being as an extraordinary product of itself.[5] So religious is the emphasis of these self-help programs that the Massachusetts legislature has even granted tax-free status to the Option Institute as a religious organization.

Prayer

Prayer is an essential feature of worship, and it figures prominently, although disguised, in most self-help programs. Daily affirmations and positive self-talk bear a striking resemblance to ritual prayer. In the religion of self-help, I do not pray to God, "Give us this day our daily bread." I pray to myself, "I am creating abundance in every area of my life. Everything I need is available for me to enjoy." I do not ask God, "Forgive us our debts (or sins or trespasses) as we forgive our debtors." I pray to myself, "I am allowing myself and others room to fail. When I fail, I forgive myself and love myself unconditionally." It is particularly interesting to me that in the Reformed tradition especially, Christians are taught that God prays to Himself for us, because we are unable even to do so much for ourselves. Paul tells us, "the Spirit helps us in our weakness. We do not know what we ought to pray for, but the Spirit himself intercedes for us with groans that words cannot express."[6] The religion of self-help parrots even this act, with the self praying to the self.

Confession

With prayer often comes confession of sin. In the religion of self-help, the faithful confess dysfunction, disease, and victimhood, admitting to being overeaters (not gluttons), procrastinators (not slothful), sex addicts (not lustful), or workaholics (not greedy). They acknowledge that they suffer from the diseases of low self-esteem, cognitive discontent, and inappropriate emotional expression, not the sins of covetousness, envy, and anger. Individuals who fail to "confess" their problems are labeled "in denial" and are considered outside the salvation offered by self-help, in much the same way that unrepentant sinners remain outside God's grace.

Forgiveness

While in a more traditional religious milieu, confession of sin is followed by atonement and divine forgiveness, the acknowledgment of dysfunction in the religion of self-help is followed by self-forgiveness. The main goal of therapy, a Freudian psychotherapist once told me, is to help the patient forgive himself. I admit that this concept is a real stumbling block for me. After all, if the problems addressed by the self-help movement are diseases and not sins, why is forgiveness necessary? I've certainly never felt the need to forgive myself for getting a cold or needing glasses or feeling a twinge of rheumatism on a damp day. Apparently, in some way that I cannot fully comprehend, people with low self-esteem or compulsive behaviors or success-inhibiting habits need to forgive themselves as part of the healing process.

Interestingly enough, even in a religion that preaches self-forgiveness as a cardinal virtue, total selfness is not really satisfying. Theory and practice do not coincide. The irony of self-help is that the self is not really sufficient unto the self. Followers of the self-help religion rely on the work of self-improvement experts, a special class of "priests," if you will, to lead the way to salvation and renewal. The faithful may be told that they need only to forgive themselves, but without the group, they lack the external assurance people need to prove they have been truly redeemed. So in the final analysis, salvation is not really possible for the self by the self. If it were, there would be no need of recovery groups or motivational speakers or success books.

Sacred readings

Scripture reading and study is a standard feature of religious worship, and it is encouraged by religious leaders as an important aspect of private devotions. Reading our sacred texts reminds us of what we believe and how we are to live our lives. The ritual of worship in self-help also includes the reading of sacred texts—that is, self-help literature or self-written creeds, affirmations, goals, and journals. Self-help promoters tell the initiates to commit their goals to paper, to write down their feelings and their positive affirmations, and then read them aloud daily or even several times a day. These promoters also recommend that self-seekers read and re-read self-improvement books. Mike Murdock, writing a typical admonition, tells his followers to read his success book at least weekly for the first several months that they're involved in his program.[7]

Memorial practices

Even nonliturgical churches practice some recurring memorial rites that involve physical actions. In the typical Baptist church, we see the Lord's Supper and baptism practiced on a regular basis. In many liturgical churches we have mass, infant baptism, confirmation, and first Communion. Other Christian practices may include ritual fasting, the imposition of ashes, and attending the stations of the cross. In the Jewish tradition we see ritual feasts and fasts, days of prayer and atonement, the mikvah, the bar mitzvah, and the bat mitzvah.

What of the self-help religion? Can it really be said to practice similar physical rites? Os Guinness has observed that people who practice the daily worship of physical perfection, as they proceed from one Nautilus machine to another, look like nothing so much as penitents walking the stations of the cross.[8] As Christians try symbolically to take on the suffering of Christ, so the self-help seekers practice the "no pain, no gain" of their religion. And in place of the communion bread and wine, we see exercise groups drinking mineral water and sharing rice cakes as they light candles and center themselves in preparation for aerobic workouts.[9]

Gnosticism

In the final analysis, the new religion of self-help is the old religion of gnosticism. (The serpent may have shed his old scales, but the new scales are made of the same, heretical stuff.) Gnostic teaching included a secret knowledge. Self-help writers promise the "secrets" of success or happiness or fulfillment. Gnostic teaching included a belief that the soul, apart from the corrupt human body, was perfect and part of the divine realm to which it would eventually return. Self-help writers tell us that perfection is our natural state, that we are divine, that the god or goddess in us only needs to be recognized. Gnosticism rejected the moral teachings of the Old Testament, saying these were created by the evil demiurge to cripple and entrap human beings. Self-esteem writers warn us about toxic religions that would shame us with their "thou shalt nots."

The modern gnostic self-help religion stands as both a danger to and an indictment of modern American Christians. It is dangerous because it is so superficially beautiful, so seductive that the church has taken it to bed and allowed herself to be infected with its retrovirus. This virus, true to its nature, is commandeering the church's reproductive machinery to replicate itself, and it is attenuating the church's ability to combat the infection of heresy. And so we see churches rewriting the Gospel to fit the self-help message, reimagining God as Sophia, reinterpreting the Ten Commandments as a recipe for human affirmation, recasting Jesus Christ in the role of archetypal business tycoon. In sexually graphic imagery, Ezekiel wrote about the effects of such an alliance between God's people and the pagan world. What makes us think that we will fare any better than Oholah and Oholibah?[10]

Perhaps worse, the self-help religion indicts Christians for failing to communicate the Gospel to a culture losing its ability to recognize truth. So completely have we failed to communicate biblical and theological truth that Jewish atheist and religious critic Harold Bloom can write that Christ became incarnate so that God could share human suffering, not so we could share God's joy.[11] Clearly, Christians have failed miserably if a man of Bloom's apparent intellect and discernment can have so completely missed the point.

But the modern hunger for truth remains, rather in the way that the desire for food continues long after the starving person is too debilitated to be able to eat. Actress Ali MacGraw acknowledged this hunger when trying to explain the success of her "Yoga Mind and Body" video, saying that our materialist society is desperately searching for the bigger picture.[12] If Christians do not provide the big picture of God, Satan in the guise of the self-help movement is only too ready to provide lots of little pictures of lots of little gods in you and me and everyone else. It may not be the big picture, but at least it's not a blank.

11

Life Behind
Enemy Lines

Christians live in enemy-occupied territory. We are constantly besieged by the forces of secularization and modernity. These forces, often in the form of self-help materials and self-help thinking, have gained a considerable foothold in many American churches, affecting education programs, worship services, and outreach campaigns. In some churches, it is becoming increasingly difficult to see past the slick marketing or the self-improvement courses to the message of the Gospel. Concerned about revenues and "relevance," some churches have even changed the Gospel to make it more palatable for late twentieth-century Americans. In the process, Christians are losing credibility, and our witness to the world is threatened.

While I am not suggesting that all the church's problems are caused by the self-help movement, I am saying that the attitudes, the thought processes, the style of self-help is so pervasive and unchallenged in our culture that Christians are bound to be influenced. Christian thought and behavior have been shaped by self-help ideas, which are insidious because of their plausibility. It is easy, for example, to identify the danger in modern secular entertainment with its violence, its sexual exploitation, and its vulgarity. Even the unredeemed have recognized and sounded warnings about harmful television, movies, and music. It is not so easy to recognize the danger in programs that promote self-esteem, positive thinking, self-improvement, wellness, or maximizing one's time and talents. Nevertheless, as we have seen, self-help is dangerous, because at its heart is the lie of Satan that we can be our own gods. This lie has infected our churches and is changing American Christianity, including evangelicalism which, as theologian David Wells has observed, "has shown itself to be a religious tradition with an enormous capacity to adapt to the cultural climate."[1]

TRUTH OR PRACTICALITY?

First and foremost, self-help has encouraged the sacrifice of truth to practicality. In the milieu of self-help, we never ask, "Is it true?" but only, "Does it work?" In the same way, practicality has become the standard for judging the church's programs. Our worship services are "seeker-friendly" because this model works for getting people into the church. Our pastors preach wholeness and healing for the inner child, not repentance and atonement for the sinner, because this kinder, gentler message works at keeping people in the church. Theology is abandoned because it isn't practical. Modern evangelicals, embracing this paradigm, insist on straining everything, theology included, "through the sieve of what appears to be 'practical,' so that what is felt becomes as important as what is known or believed."[2] What has happened to truth?

Many of the new megachurches are obvious examples of the power of practical thinking. In their quest for success, as defined by size, they have canonized what Os Guinness has called "the Holy Family of the spiritual, the relational, and the practical."[3] Consumed with a "bottom-line" mentality, a kind of religious accountancy, these megachurches emphasize "statistics and data at the expense of truth."[4] Church growth experts even make the bald-faced assertion that in order to build congregations, church leaders must remember that "the audience, not the message, is sovereign."[5] Coupled with audience sovereignty is the further belief that ideas are legitimate only when they prove valuable in the religious marketplace. "Evangelicals have been willing to bestow legitimacy only on ideas that *work*," writes David Wells.[6] What has happened to truth?

Church-sponsored self-help groups are replacing formal Christian doctrine with ideas devised by group consensus. These ideas allow the group to redefine the meaning of sacred texts, of prayer, even of God. Most religious small groups, writes Robert Wuthnow, "do not assert the value of denominational traditions or pay much attention to distinctive theological arguments that have identified variants of Christianity or Judaism in the past. Indeed, many of the groups encourage faith to be subjective and pragmatic."[7] What has happened to truth?

Louis Farrakhan's Million Man March of October 16, 1995, is a glaring example of the abandonment of truth. Black Christian leaders, men such as Jesse Jackson and Joseph Lowery, flocked to Farrakhan because they believed that his message was practical, that his plan would work; black men would begin to behave responsibly. But in the process of this compromise, Christianity was made to appear as just one more ideology, no different from Islam. And Louis Farrakhan was portrayed as just one more charismatic leader, no different from Martin Luther King, Jr.

In their pursuit of the practical, black Christian men chose to ignore Farrakhan's diatribes against the Jews, whom he continues to berate as "bloodsuckers." They chose to ignore Farrakhan's self-aggrandizing claim to be another Moses, sent on a special mission by the direct word of God. They chose to ignore Farrakhan's arrogant assertion that he *is* the Dream. (Martin Luther King, Jr., only *had* a dream.) They chose to ignore the militant stand of Islam, with its goal to eradicate Christianity and Judaism. They chose to ignore the fact that Hitler's reign began with just such a sacrifice of truth to practicality. (The Germans might not have approved of Hitler, but at least his methods worked. Germany got back on its economic feet.) And Christians who continue to applaud the Million Man March have chosen to ignore Farrakhan's recent summit meeting with world terrorist Muammar el-Qaddafi. What has happened to truth?

GOSPEL OR GROWTH?

Once you abandon truth and embrace the practical, it is possible to justify any means as long as the ends are acceptable. But how acceptable are the ends currently being pursued by our churches, both evangelical and mainline? The purpose of man—his end, if you will—is to "glorify God and enjoy him forever." But the ends of many churches and televangelists today are the ends of self-help: self-affirmation, self-esteem, wholeness, and unlimited prosperity. In an analysis of Christian broadcasting, communications professor Quentin Schultze noted that Christian television seems to focus far more on entertainment and money than on the Gospel. According to Schultze, positive thinking and name-it-and-claim-it messages have often replaced the Gospel.[8] A case in point is *The 700 Club*, which heavily promotes Pat Robertson's seemingly endless line of products, from his books to his conferences to his university. And who hasn't heard about the scandal of Jim Bakker's quest for money and power?

Some of this same prosperity message is insinuating itself even in churches that usually decry such self-serving ministries. Pastors who preach uncompromisingly against the prosperity gospel will still invoke Malachi to encourage tithing in their churches, promising their congregations that tithing will bring rich rewards. "'Bring the whole tithe into the storehouse, that there may be food in my house. Test me in this,' says the Lord Almighty, 'and see if I will not throw open the floodgates of heaven and pour out so much blessing that you will not have room enough for it.'"[9] But by using Scripture in this way, pastors tacitly imply that we give in order to get.

Other church leaders, drawing from the pop psychology that

sustains the recovery movement, feed their congregations homilies on healing, not suffering. Theologian David Wells has observed that "we evangelicals are feasting on the crumbs under the psychologists' table and trying to make a meal of it. You hear it in the language, where being good is translated into feeling good. We're getting a Christianity that is more interested in wholeness than in holiness."[10] A prime example is Robert Schuller, who proudly proclaims that he appeals to our need for dignity rather than focusing his ministry on human shame.[11] Tim Stafford, writing in *Christianity Today*, warned that this trend "could be a secularizing force, smuggling non-Christian ideas into the church. It might produce an amoral, unchallenged people, for whom religion is a form of self-congratulation. It might be the guise under which theological liberalism finally conquers orthodoxy: humanity and its 'needs' becoming the measure of all things, God being reduced to a source of comfort and inspiration."[12] I would change Stafford's conditional "might" to a certain "is."

THE GREAT COMMISSION OR AN ENCOUNTER GROUP?

While Jesus sent His followers into the world with the command that they preach the Gospel and make disciples, self-help draws us inward to the small group and eventually to the even smaller self. So important have small self-help groups become in our churches that membership in them has surpassed adult Sunday school involvement.[13]

Proponents of small groups insist that they help people look deeper into their faith. But could it be that many groups simply make people *feel* like disciples without requiring true discipleship and all its inevitable pain and sacrifice? Robert Wuthnow, who spent many years studying the small group phenomenon in America, concluded that these church-sponsored groups "do little to increase biblical knowledge. Indeed, many of the groups encourage faith to be subjective and pragmatic. . . . It does not overstate the case to suggest that the small group movement is currently playing a major role in *adapting* American religion to the main currents of secular culture."[14] And some critics charge that today's small groups are more concerned "with the emotional state of the individual than with spiritual formulation; some are prone to accent subjective experiences more than objective truths."[15] Theologian J. I. Packer has suggested that making Christian friends, not seeking God, is the real goal of church small groups.[16]

But in the final analysis, small groups, in church or out, may not even be about friendships. Sometimes they are simply another way to satisfy the self. Members of these groups may call each other a family, but what family ever worked the way a small group does? "The social contract binding members together asserts only the weakest obligations. Come if you have time. Talk if you feel like it. Respect everyone's opinion. Never criticize. Leave quietly if you become dissatisfied. Families would never survive by following these operating norms," wrote Robert Wuthnow, who sagely observed that "some small groups merely provide occasions for individuals to focus on themselves in the presence of others."[17]

GOD OR SOPHIA OR ME?

When you abandon the orthodox truth of Christianity, it becomes possible to replace the one holy Triune God with a god of one's own making. Robert Schuller has succeeded masterfully in convincing his audience that we should replace our outmoded God-centered theology with a human-centered theology of self-esteem. Not everyone who wishes to remake God is as bold, as forthright about it as Schuller. They disguise their program under the auspices of making God more relevant or more accessible or more user-friendly to today's seekers, as if God were some IBM or Microsoft product. (*Is your old God too hard to utilize? Plug in to our new seeker-friendly version. Now available on CD-ROM.*)

But however you may disguise your intentions, the end result is the same. Gone is the transcendent God, the complete Other, who stands outside and apart from the creation that He called forth from nothing, simply by speaking. Gone is the God of absolute truth and righteousness, the God who would be worthy of our worship because of what He is, quite apart from what He does. Gone is the God whose goodness is so absolute, so hard, so brilliant that we can only prostrate ourselves before it; we cannot bear to face it. Gone is the God whose throne is surrounded by mighty creatures, covered with eyes, adorned by wings, who praise God ceaselessly. This God is dangerous. He casts a stark and revealing light on the utterly insignificant self that the self-help movement puts so much stock in. This God, if self-help is to succeed at selling us the god of self, must go.

What are we left with? If we are lucky, we have the anemic, emasculated Jesus of third-rate pietistic paintings. The sweet Jesus who called little children to His side and told us to love each other. Jesus our brother, meek and mild. The Jesus who, as Dorothy Sayers so rightly observed, is fit only for old ladies and pale curates.

And if we're not so lucky? The wishy-washy Jesus is supplanted by the "spirit" of Jesus in myself. And from there, it is only a very small step to replacing any last vestige of Jesus with myself alone—the divine in me, the god Me. After all, didn't Jesus tell me that the kingdom of God is inside of me? Am I not part of the image of God? And so we see that little by little, the gnostic heresy that lies at the heart of self-help insinuates itself into American Christianity. Our essence, our soul, our self becomes divinely perfect and preexistent with God, worthy of all worship and praise.

It is this willingness to remake God, to recast ourselves as gods, that lies behind what is surely one of the most appalling displays of heresy in recent years—the 1993 Re-Imagining God conference. Supported and attended by women from thirty-two denominations and twenty-seven countries, the conference attacked what was portrayed as a chauvinistic view of God intended to enslave and degrade women. Worse, God was called an abusive parent, orthodox Christianity a violent theology, and the atonement of Jesus "weird."[18] Of course, this charge is not new, as C. S. Lewis reminds in *The Pilgrim's Regress:* "In these latter days there is no charge against the Landlord which the Enemy brings so often as cruelty."[19]

In the place of this dangerous God, Re-Imagining attenders named Sophia as our maker, and they celebrated female sexuality with an incantation that smacked of pagan fertility rites. (Incidentally, Sophia was a gnostic deity.) Further, the women at Re-Imagining denied the transcendence of God and affirmed their right to restructure theology according to their own experiences and understandings. God is what I decide him to be. I make God. I unmake gods. Blessing and glory be to Me.

THE BIBLE OR CHRISTIAN LIVING?

Once we accept the new gods of self-help—the gods of self—we need to find new scriptures to study them. After all, what does the Bible tell us about the self other than that it is desperately wicked and sinful, that it is the enemy of God, that it is incapable of righteousness? What we need are books that tell us how to build the self, encourage the self, fulfill the self, comfort the self, protect the self, provide for the self, and honor the self in ourselves and others.

Glory be to Self, such books exist. They are called "Christian living" books. Versions of these books are issued by most Christian publishing houses, and they have flooded Christian bookstores, libraries, and classrooms. As a writer and an avid reader, I receive regular mailings from a good half-dozen Christian book clubs. Without exception, these clubs offer more "Christian living" than any other single category of books. And at the 1995 Christian Booksellers Convention in Denver, there were hundreds of titles under the category of success alone. This trend is not new. A 1983 analysis of eight evangelical presses revealed that 87.8 percent of their books dealt with self-help topics.[20]

Now don't get me wrong. Christian living books are not necessarily idolatrous in themselves. Many are thoughtful, biblical, and helpful in encouraging Christians and providing solutions to contemporary problems. But, as Baptist minister and sociology Professor Anthony Campolo has observed, they often distort the Gospel and present Christianity as a kind of psychotherapy rather than as Jesus' call to radical discipleship.[21] These books either ignore or criticize such outmoded, unpopular concepts as sacrifice, duty, and charity. Instead, they encourage self-affirmation, self-acceptance, time management, and wise investment. Furthermore, they draw us away from any serious engagement of the intellect, critical studies of theology, in-depth Bible exegesis, and a search for understanding and truth.

SACRIFICE OR SELF?

The model of love that God presents in Scripture is one of sacrifice. No sacrifice, not even that of an only Son, is too great to ask or to give as an expression of love. Furthermore, God shows us that sacrificial love is to be acted out in the context of total submission and humility. After all, the sacrifice can hardly be laudable if I am aware of my sacrifice and I make others aware of it, too. We all know how truly annoying a "martyr" can be. When we are called to sacrifice, we are not called to be Patience on a Monument, but lovers. The act is positive, not negative.

Jesus humbled Himself unto death. The Holy Spirit acts with such utter humility that His work always makes us see the glory of Jesus Christ more clearly, not the Holy Spirit. And God is always willing to take us on terms that no human pride would be willing to endure. Howard Snyder, Professor of Evangelism and Church Renewal at United Theological Seminary, put it this way: "Father, Son, and Holy Spirit love each other unreservedly and without limit. But the condition for their aggregate love is their mutual submission and self-giving."[22]

Submission and self-giving are unpopular concepts with the self-help movement. More than that, they are considered psychologically harmful. This attitude has found a home in Christian churches where classes on self-esteem are more popular than classes on Paul, where forgiveness is offered without repentance, where salvation can be had without the Cross.

But this popular bias against selflessness has consequences that even the secular world is beginning to realize, to its credit. Writing in *The Wall Street Journal*, an assistant attorney general for Arizona, Andrew Peyton Thomas, warned, "Self-centeredness and its related vices—crime, illegitimacy, child neglect—are exploding in America because, after centuries of Western philosophy devoted to the purpose, Americans are glorifying extreme individualism beyond healthy limits." It is interesting that Mr. Thomas offers a solution right out of orthodox Christianity: "There are two things that would solve all of our so-called social problems, neither of which can be legislated. These are self-denial and love."[23]

RADICAL DISCIPLESHIP OR CHEAP GRACE?

The call of Jesus Christ is the call to radical discipleship. It is the call to obedience to the person of Jesus Christ. It is the call that commands us to die to the self. Dietrich Bonhoeffer explained it this way: "When Christ calls a man, he bids him come and die. It may be a death like that of the first disciples, or it may be a death like that of Luther's, who had to leave the monastery and go out into the world. But it is the same death every time—death in Jesus Christ, the death of the old man at his call."[24]

To respond to Christ's call, however, does not mean simply that we deny ourselves, rather that we become so aware of Christ that we forget all about ourselves. "Self-denial is never just a series of isolated acts of mortification or asceticism. It is not suicide, for there is an element of self-will even in that. To deny oneself is to be aware only of Christ and no more of self," Bonhoeffer tells us.[25]

Radical discipleship that denies the self stands in direct opposition to self-help's teaching, which insists that we must explore the self, find the self, and fulfill the self. In the church, self-help teaching has taken on a veneer of spirituality by telling us that we can love God and others only when we learn to love the self first. And what is the nature of that self? According to self-help thinking, that self is a glorious thing, because it is created in the image of God. It is worthy of unconditional love because God saves it by grace. Lewis B. Smedes, Professor of Integrative Studies at Fuller Theological Seminary, has written that we are actually *worthy* of the grace of salvation, contradicting orthodox Christian theology but affirming self-help teaching.[26] But as C. S. Lewis so wisely pointed out, "No creature that deserved redemption would need to be redeemed. Christ died for men precisely because men are not worth dying for."[27]

You can see the selfishness of self-help thinking being acted out in churches all across America. From petty internal bickering to all-out doctrinal warfare between denominations, the focus on self is damaging the body of Christ. People look for churches that offer the cheap grace of affirmation; they leave churches that expect discipleship. My most unpleasant experience as a Presbyterian elder was listening to a letter from a woman who was leaving the church because she felt it had nothing to give her as a single parent. I could not understand why she had never asked how she could serve the church, only how the church could serve her. Sadly, this woman's attitude is not an exception.

The saving grace of self-help, the view of grace that has found its way into our churches, is what Bonhoeffer has called cheap grace. "Cheap grace means grace as a doctrine, as principle, as system. It means forgiveness of sins proclaimed as a general truth, the love of God taught as the 'conception' of God," Bonhoeffer wrote.[28] This view of grace leads inevitably to a belief, common among many religious self-help proponents, that the Incarnation's purpose was to help us know and appreciate ourselves better.

The challenge for the church today is to rediscover radical discipleship, to teach that there is a difference between the Christian life and the life that Bonhoeffer called "bourgeois respectability."[29] The Christian life is only possible when Christ, not the self, is firmly fixed at the center of our lives; when Christ, not the self, is the measure of all things; when Christ, not the self, is the Alpha and Omega of our existence.

12

Withstanding the Enemy's Lies

I believe that it is the writer's chief responsibility to observe and comment on the society in which he or she lives, not to offer solutions to society's problems. Writers, like all artists, raise questions that they are not necessarily required to answer. The goal is to make the reader think. Nevertheless, there are things we can and should do as Christians to arm ourselves against the seductive lies of the self-help movement. So at the risk of stepping outside the role of social commentator, I humbly offer my suggestions here.

STUDY THE BIBLE

Our first line of defense against the enemy's lies is the holy Scripture. Jesus Himself used the Word of God to withstand the attacks of Satan, and Paul counseled Timothy, saying, "All Scripture is God-breathed and is useful for teaching, rebuking, correcting and training in righteousness, so that the man of God may be thoroughly equipped for every good work."[1] And in one of his many confrontations with the Sadducees, Jesus tells them that they fall into error because they do not know the Scriptures— a serious charge to be leveled at any learned Jew. Even Jesus' accu-

sation, "Have you not read what God said to you," was harsher
than the usual appeal made by Jewish disputants, who would tell
their opponents to "go and read" a section of God's Word to ostensibly settle an argument. In making His charge, Jesus was not only
reinforcing the importance of Scripture in the lives of God's chosen people, but accusing those people of neglecting their duty to
God in not immersing themselves in its study.[2]

Jesus' charge is even more convicting today. American
Christians, both mainline and evangelical, have a serious gap in
their knowledge of the Bible. According to a recent Gallup poll,
basic Bible knowledge is at an all-time low, despite the fact that
eight out of ten Americans claim to be Christians. George Gallup,
whose company has been following religious trends for about fifty
years, has commented that Americans don't know what they
believe or why. Gallup also believes that biblical illiteracy is a serious spiritual, religious, and cultural problem in America.[3] Indiana
University president and ethics professor, Thomas Ehrlich,
agrees. He has observed that very few college students today have
grown up reading the Bible.[4]

As bad as biblical illiteracy is, the misuse of Scripture is a far
more serious problem. It is one thing simply to be ignorant of the
Word of God; it is quite another to distort it. The first shortcom-
ing affects only the person who lives in ignorance. The second can
affect everyone who hears and may be influenced by the distorted
interpretation, both the redeemed and, worse, the lost.

Distortion of Scripture is a common tactic among self-help
writers, Christian and non-Christian alike. One Christian self-
help writer tells us to listen carefully to God's Word, and we will
hear God say that He likes who we are.[5] Another Christian success writer quotes randomly from the Old and New Testaments
to prove that Jesus was a master salesman who has given us the
tools for wealth and achievement.[6] Still another tells us that the
real challenge of the Bible is not to give but to receive love.[7] And
one non-Christian self-help writer has interpreted the words of
Jesus, "Blessed are the pure in heart for they shall see God," to

mean that people who purify their consciousness will see themselves as God.[8] And just about every proponent of positive thinking quotes the King James version of Proverbs 23:7 to prove that "what you think about, you bring about."

"Manipulative use of the Bible for self-interest runs like a river through the history of the church. Today such abuse has turned into a flood," writes New Testament scholar G. Walter Hansen, who warns, "If we only use the Bible as a mirror to see ourselves, we may wind up seeing more of a reflection of our own self-interests than a revelation of God's interests."[9]

But before we cast stones at the self-help movement for this abuse, we need to ask ourselves if we are similarly guilty. How many Bible study classes have you attended in which the leader has asked, "What does this passage mean to *you*?" How many times have you led a class and asked that very question? The problem with this question is that it fails to make the necessary distinction between meaning and personal significance. Bible scholar Walt Russell has explained this distinction: "The meaning of a text never changes. In contrast, the significance of that text to me and to others is very fluid and flexible. By confusing these two aspects of the interpretation process, we evangelicals approach the Bible with an *interpretive relativism*. If it means one thing to you and something contradictory to me, we have no ultimate court of appeal. We can never establish and validate the one correct interpretation."[10]

Relativism? I can think of no charge that evangelicals would find more personally distasteful. Indeed, evangelicals regularly rail against the relativism of modern society, modern morality, modern ethics, and modern truth. But consider these statistics from a Barna Research Group survey. When questioned about absolute truth, 66 percent of adult Americans (and a whopping 72 percent of Americans aged eighteen to twenty-five) responded that absolute truth does not exist. Most Americans today believe that people can disagree about truth and still be correct.[11] Considering the number of Americans who claim to be evangelicals, it seems clear that there must be one or two who reject absolute truth and, logically, Jesus' claim to be that truth.

In their eagerness to make Scripture meaningful to the individual, to find personal and immediate life applications, evangelicals often ignore the historical, cultural, and literary context of a passage or chapter or whole book of Scripture. "In believing that God's Word directly addresses us, we ignore that he speaks to our needs *through* the historical and literary contexts of people of the Bible," says Walt Russell.[12] Theologian Thomas Oden has echoed this view, observing that some evangelicals "have fixated upon 'me and the Bible, and especially me,' so that what Bible reading becomes is primarily an assertion of inward feelings."[13]

So how should we study the Bible? First, we need to study the Bible for itself, not for our own felt needs. We should ask, "What does the Bible say?" not, "What does it say to me?" If I study the Bible looking for proof that God wants me to be happy or successful or whole or fulfilled, you can be sure that I will find it, because my mind-set will determine my interpretation of Scripture. When I read the Bible with my felt needs in mind, I strip Scripture of any objective truth. All that remains is a gooey relativism that changes as my circumstances, mood, and needs change. Reading Scripture subjectively elevates my context over that of the Bible. This perspective, Russell maintains, is dangerous because "it presupposes an existential and human-centered world view."[14]

But this is exactly the presupposition upon which self-help thinking rests, the belief that I exist for myself and that, if God exists at all, He exists to help me see myself more clearly and in a more positive light. This is exactly the presupposition that Robert Schuller endorses when he insists that we need a human-centered theology. This is the worldview that reduces God to a cosmic reliever of our existential angst and the Gospel to a recipe for our personal progress and enlightenment and fulfillment. In the self-help context, Scripture does not exist as God's revelation of Himself to us. Scripture exists to help us understand ourselves.

But even a study of Scripture that focuses on our quest for discipleship can become self-serving and self-centered. As Christians, we need to read the Bible for what it is, not for what it can do for us. We study the Word of God because it is the Word of God, because it proceeds from the sublime Other who is the object of our greatest passion, our most intense desire.

I remember the love that seemed to overwhelm me when each of my children was born. As they grew, I would spend hours just watching them, studying every gesture, learning every mannerism, delighting in their emerging personalities, their distinctive turns of minds, their particular expressions of thought. I wanted to know my children, not because of what they could give me, not even because I wanted to become a better mother, but simply because I loved them.

Our love for God should be so much greater. Our desire for Him should be such a consuming passion that we want to know everything possible about Him. Yes, we study the Bible to learn discipleship, but such a study is dry bones compared to the passionate study we should make of our Love, simply because we love Him and we desire to be close to Him.

Our goal, then, is to keep the self, as much as possible, out of our Bible study. We need to remember that God's Word is truth, that God wants to reveal Himself to us, and that all Scripture has a meaning that the Author intended. To find that truth, to understand God's revelation, we need to study the Bible objectively, which includes both exegetical investigations and research into the cultural, historical, and literary context of Scripture. As we approach each book of the Bible, we need to find out everything we can about the inspired human author—his life, his times, his purpose in writing the book, his readers. We need to find out if the book serves as prophecy, history, or poetry. We need to understand how the book was put together and what its major themes are.

Because we don't have the original autographs of Scripture (and few of us could read them if we did), we need to read the Bible in translation. The translation you choose will probably be a matter of personal taste and background. Just keep in mind that all of the translations have advantages; all have shortcomings. Sometimes we gain new insights by reading a new translation. In any event, we should remember: "The religious problems of the world are not caused by people reading different translations; the most serious problem is that many people read no translation!"[15]

Whatever translation you choose, it helps to use a "study" version of that translation. Study Bibles typically include the type of background information described above. You should also have an exhaustive concordance, which helps with in-depth exegesis, and as many good Bible commentaries as you can afford or can borrow from a library, friend, or pastor.

Just a brief word on commentaries. Historically, evangelicals have exhibited a bias against authority. Rooted in democratic populism, the evangelical movement has often stressed the ability of Everyman to interpret Scripture. While independent Bible study can be fruitful, I believe in consulting the work of trained Bible scholars who have dedicated their lives to studying the oldest texts available and to clarifying the meaning and truth of Scripture. God has called scholars to this sacred task, and I believe it is a foolish waste of time to ignore their work.

STUDY CHURCH HISTORY

Thomas Oden observed that the overwhelming evangelical focus on personal experience in Bible study "has sadly prevented readers from . . . learning that the Spirit has a history, and that the body of Christ being called forth in that history has unity. . . . Beware of the 'evangelical' who wants to read the Bible without the historic voices of the church, who is only willing to listen to his own voice or the voices of contemporaries in the dialogue. Evangelicals have usually been the losers when they have systematically neglected the saints and martyrs and consensual writers of the earliest Christian centuries."[16] What Oden is saying is that evangelical Christians need to learn about church history and the work of great Christian writers, theologians, and scholars whose work can tell us at least as much, if not more, about biblical truth and meaning as the work of modern interpreters.

Many American evangelicals approach Christianity as if correct doctrine and true devotion to Christ can be found only within the modern evangelical movement. There is a deep suspicion of Roman Catholicism and even of mainline Protestant denominations where, many evangelicals feel, hardly a "real" Christian can be found. This attitude has led, sadly, to a disturbing ignorance of church history, its significant movements and its great leaders.

By ignoring the past, we doom ourselves to repeat its mistakes endlessly. Gnosticism, for example, has threatened Christianity from its earliest days. If we do not study our past, we will not recognize contemporary manifestations, often appearing in self-help literature, of this old enemy. And Pelagianism, the belief that man's nature is essentially good and that man can perfect himself by his own efforts, is precisely the philosophy that self-help teaches. When we do not understand our past, we have trouble recognizing our old enemy in his new scales.

And by failing to study church history, we are forced always to reinvent the wheel, to rethink Christian doctrine, to redefine orthodoxy. We fail to recognize that the truth of Christianity is a truth that is timeless. It is the same yesterday, today, and forever. By studying church history, we acknowledge this timeless quality of Christian truth, and we infuse our understanding with an element that transcends our time-bound thinking, our late-twentieth-century parochialism that insists that "newer is better."

Furthermore, it is only by studying our past that we catch even a glimpse of the Church's real, eternal nature. Existing in time as we do, we can see only a tiny shadow of the Church. Existing outside of time, God sees the Church stretching back through the centuries to the first apostles and on into the future where she is reunited with Christ. This is the Church that God uses and of which we are a part. We are not alone as the Church in this place on the river of time. We are connected to our Christian brothers and sisters in all times, and for all time, in a continuity of adoration for God and commitment to Christ that gives the Church its strength. By studying our past, we can marshal that strength to protect our beliefs from the onslaught of self-centered self-help that would convince us to recreate the church to meet modern needs. But our needs are not modern. They are the needs of all Christians through all time. They are the needs to know God, to be saved by His grace, and to dwell with Him and for Him eternally.

In the same way, studying the lives of Church leaders offers us real heroes rather than the secular heroes of self-help. No Tony Robbins or Stephen Covey here, but men and women who lived out the teachings of Scripture in giving themselves in loving submission to Jesus Christ, to the holy Church, and to each other. And the writings of these Christian giants illuminate the Scriptures with an understanding and acceptance of truth that we cannot afford to ignore.

Believing in the total trustworthiness of Scripture, for example, is not a modern theological viewpoint, as many evangelicals seem to believe. Gregory of Nyssa and St. Augustine both affirmed that Scripture speaks with the voice of God. Timothy George, dean of Beeson Divinity School, underscores the importance of returning to the works of our Christian fathers, noting, "The massive consensus of thoughtful Christian interpretation of the Word down the ages (and on most matters of importance there is such a thing) is not likely to be wrong."[17]

STUDY CHURCH CREEDS

Evangelical churches tend to be noncreedal, believing that all statements of faith must be subservient to the Scriptures. Certainly Scripture always takes precedence, but ignoring the traditional creeds has led to the age-old problem of throwing out the baby with the bath water. Worse, by ignoring the creeds, we make the arrogant assumption that the Holy Spirit somehow abandoned the church after the death of the apostles.

Formal statements of faith serve a vital function for believers. The traditional creeds help protect orthodoxy. They were not written by one or two people to express personal opinions about doctrine or about Scripture. Nor were these creeds written to shock believers with their uncompromising and fearless quest for the latest interpretation of the nature and meaning of divinity, which is frequently the case with modern, particularly liberal, theological works. These creeds were written to clarify biblical truth and to save the church from heresy and apostasy. They were formulated by gatherings of great church leaders and Bible scholars, generally in debate over a serious problem or disagreement that had arisen within the church.

The Council of Nicaea, for example, met in A.D. 325 to settle disagreements over the triune nature of God and the divinity of Christ. Because of Nicaea, the heresy of Arianism, which asserted that Jesus Christ was a created being and, therefore, not truly divine, was defeated. Because of Nicaea, we affirm today that the Lord Jesus Christ is the "only begotten Son of God; begotten of His Father before all worlds; God of God; Light of Light; Very God of Very God; Begotten, not made; Being of one substance with the Father." These words, with their theological richness and their glorious affirmation of the eternal existence of Jesus, who is of the same substance—*homoousios*—as God, should not be discarded or ignored by modern evangelicals simply because they do not belong to the canon of Scripture.

The Council at Nicaea, like those following it, checked the heresies that denied the Trinity, the divinity of the Holy Ghost, the dual nature of Christ as perfect God and perfect man, and the physical resurrection of Jesus. When we ignore the creeds these councils formulated, we do so to our own peril.

For example, consider the work of Douglas F. Ottati, professor of theology at Union Theological Seminary in Virginia. Ottati claims that the New Testament is not history but narrative and symbolic thematization. Jesus Christ, in this context, is a "symbolic form," a "mundane medium of revelation," an "illustration of grace," or a "God-shaped man." Ottati denounces the Chalcedonian Definition of 451 that "Jesus Christ is actually God and actually man" as flawed doctrine. Ottati and others like him apparently feel free to reinterpret Scripture to serve their purposes. And their work is sufficiently compelling that they are able to convert many to their beliefs. But they cannot reformulate the ancient creeds. How do you reinterpret the statement that Jesus Christ was begotten of the Father? The value of the creeds is their very straightforward nature. They must be either accepted or denied. And so Ottati denies them. But by doing so, he shows that he has broken with orthodox Christianity, broken with Christians down through history, broken with the revealed truth of God.

Studying the creeds also reminds us that, as the ecclesiast wrote, "there is nothing new under the sun."[18] The heresies of gnosticism, Arianism, Pelagianism, and Manichaeism remain with us today. We can see them in works of modern self-help writers and of liberal theologians who insist on calling themselves Christians while worshiping a pantheon of pagan gods, not the least of which is the god (or goddess) Self. Our church fathers and mothers struggled against these same heresies. In every generation, the serpent is the same, although his scales may be new. And so again we are linked to past Christians, as future Christians will be linked to us, in the great struggle against the enemy. Creeds remind us that this war is not new, and they encourage us to remain faithful and to take up our arms daily.

Finally, we need to remember that faith statements, such as the Apostles' Creed, were originally worded to begin: "We believe," not "I believe." In reciting creeds, we identify ourselves with the total faith and experience of the Church, according to Dr. William Barclay.[19] This has often been a sticking point for evangelicals, who have traditionally concentrated on the personal experience of faith in Christ to the exclusion of the experience of the faith community. While it is true that each individual person needs to accept Jesus Christ as Lord and Savior, the overwhelming emphasis on radical individualism leaves evangelicalism open to charges of gnosticism. In any event, we need to remind ourselves and each other that God's revelation of Himself "was handed down to us through a community created by covenant with God."[20] It is not for nothing that Christians are commanded to seek each other out for worship and work in communities. The writer of Hebrews, in language typical of Jewish writers of the day, warned against individualism, against a spirit of separatism. Believers were told to worship together. Those who did not would ultimately fall away and be lost.[21]

STUDY APOLOGETICS

C. S. Lewis was led first to belief in God and then to faith in Christ through a process of reason and logic. He spent the rest of his life defending his faith by clearly spelling out its logical consistency and compelling truthfulness. His apologetic was, if I may use a rather unpopular term, manly. (But then I think women can be as manly as men.) His defense of Christianity was vigorous, powerful, and forthright. It was free of the pietistic, evangelical jargon that alienates rather than enlightens the modern skeptic. By insisting and showing that Christianity makes plain sense, Lewis was able to win, as his books continue to win, thousands to Christ.

A study of Christian apologetics, the reasoned defense of Christian beliefs, can not only help us reach the unsaved, but it can help shore up our defenses against self-help and other forms of modernity. So why do so many modern Christians, evangelicals in particular, seem to be suspicious of apologetics and afraid of discussions that question our beliefs? Do they assume that Christianity defies logic and reason, that it cannot be proven, and that it must be accepted on faith alone? Do they assume that if you question Christianity, you cannot possibly believe it? Do they see apologetics as denying the role of faith in belief?

The unwillingness to enter into the logical, rational defense of our beliefs is a fairly recent development in the history of Christianity. In the early days, both Christians and pagans used reason to defend their worldviews, according to theologian Colin Brown, who has written extensively on Christianity and philosophy.[22] But with the work of theologians such as Søren Kierkegaard and Karl Barth, many Christians, intellectual and grass roots alike, began to express the opinion that man could do nothing to search rationally for God. All that man could do to save himself was to make an irrational leap of faith to reach what Francis Schaeffer called the "upper story" of nonrational belief. Belief in God, according to this view, has no basis in reason. We believe because the alternative is despair, not because the belief is Truth, not because the belief makes sense, not because the belief offers a logically consistent explanation of human history and, indeed, of all reality.

But faith is not a mindless, unreasoning emotion. When the writer of Hebrews tells us, "Faith is the substance of things hoped for, the evidence of things not seen,"[23] he is not saying that faith is irrational. And if we examine the nature of faith in our everyday lives, we will realize that it is based on reason, knowledge, and experience—not a desperate longing to believe the unbelievable simply to save ourselves from a nihilistic universe.

I have faith when I go to bed at night that the sun will rise the next morning because of my knowledge of the physical universe. (That knowledge, incidentally, rests firmly on a belief in a rational God who has created an orderly universe that follows predictable laws. Despite what postmodernists may say about a random universe, if they really believed that our cosmos was a crap shoot, they would be far more fearful of nightfall than they seem to be.) I have faith that I will be able to find my way to the grocery store because of my knowledge of local terrain. My faith in the actions of intimate acquaintances results from my knowledge of them. The better I know a person, the more faith I have in that person. Someone who has always proven to be reliable to me will engender my faith, even if he or she should tell me something quite preposterous. In the same way, the more I know about God, the more faith I will have. The more I question and find the answers of Christianity to be true, the stronger, not the weaker, my faith will be.

Christian apologist Winfried Corduan assures us, "We should never fear investigating truth."[24] Furthermore, he insists that "if Christianity is true, it should be able to withstand the hardest questions we can bring to it. If Christianity is not true, we should reject it."[25] Obviously, Corduan is not afraid to question his beliefs because he is convinced of their truth. I think that the study of Christian apologetics helps us articulate why we believe in God, why we trust in Christ, and why we choose to submit to the authority of Scripture. Apologetics helps us strengthen our beliefs and gives us more ammunition to guard ourselves and our church against the attacks of self-help thinking.

LEARN TO ACCEPT PARADOX

One of the dangers of self-help is that it looks a bit like Christianity—albeit a superficial and watered-down version with all the perilous, dark, mysterious, and demanding elements of real Christianity removed. The Christianity of self-help preaches self-forgiveness, self-affirmation, and self-worthiness. The person of Christ, if He enters into the self-help religion at all, functions as a loving, supportive brother or friend. Self-help is a religion only of consolation, good feelings, and comfort. It is a religion that appeals to our laziness because it requires of us neither troublesome discipleship nor intellectual vigor. We need not submit to the lordship of Christ. We need not study to show ourselves approved. We need only believe that we are in every way and at all times worthy of all goodness and all godness.

But this self-help religion ultimately fails to satisfy, which may be one reason why the market for new self-help books is almost limitless. People keep coming back for new books, because the old ones do not and cannot live up to their promises. Self-help, both in its overtly secular form and in its tacitly "Christian" version, doesn't satisfy because, as C. S. Lewis explained, "No real belief in the watered versions can last. Bemused and besotted as we are, we still dimly know at heart that nothing which is at all times and in every way agreeable to us can have objective reality. It is of the nature of the real that it should have sharp corners and rough edges."[26] Furthermore, as Lewis was fond of explaining, things that are truly real are quirky. They aren't what you would imagine. Christianity has just that odd spin to it that real things have. It isn't neat. It isn't simple. It certainly isn't what you would expect. It is full of darkness and mystery and paradox.

Modern believers need to accept the paradoxes of Christianity if they are to experience the fullness of God's truth and if they are to become truly armored against the easy explanations, the pat answers, the simple worldview of self-help. When self-help tells us that we have a right to put ourselves first, we must remember Christ's paradoxical saying, "So the last will be first, and the first will be last."[27] And when self-help tells us that we own ourselves, we need to remember: "Whoever finds his life will lose it, and whoever loses his life for my sake will find it."[28]

Christianity is full of such paradoxes. We have a God who is One, yet Three. We follow a Lord who was fully human and fully divine. We believe that in order to truly live, we must die; to receive, we must give; to be exalted, we must be humbled. Perhaps most disturbing of all, certainly a great stumbling block for much of modern thinking, is our central Christian belief that in order to be healed, we must be covered in blood. But not just any blood. The blood of innocence, the blood of perfection, the blood of the willing victim. What does self-help have to offer us compared with these great mysteries that through the centuries have ennobled and enlightened and elevated the men and women who, for the sake of the Author of those mysteries, were willing to be ridiculed and misunderstood and persecuted?

EVALUATE CHRISTIAN LIVING BOOKS

Every Christian bookstore I have ever entered includes a special section just for "Christian living" books. Covering topics such as marriage, parenting, single living, divorce, recovery, investment, and success, these books function in precisely the same way and appeal to the same human needs as secular self-help books. Many of these books offer useful insights and information. Others fall into the same traps and perpetuate the same half-truths and lies of secular self-help books. But even the best, focused as they ultimately are on the self, fall far short of the biblical examples of and commandments about Christian submission, self-giving, and love.

So how do we protect ourselves from the distorted views of Christian self-help writers while availing ourselves of those that help us become better servants of Christ? Here are a few suggestions:

1. Be on the lookout for the lies of self-help. When you thumb through a book, try to find out whether the author advocates happiness, success, or self-esteem as an end in itself. Does the author use God, Christianity, and Scripture as human need gratifiers? Does the author acknowledge the sinfulness of man, or are human beings portrayed as essentially good? Does the author acknowledge the prior claims of God to our persons, or does he assume that we own ourselves? Is the end of the book to glorify God or self-improvement?

2. Read critical reviews by accepted authorities. Don't assume that just because a book has been written by an author you admire or released by a Christian publishing house that its teachings are solidly Christian. Find out whether any recognized theologians or Bible scholars have reviewed the book. Then find out what they have to say about the book in light of orthodox Christian teachings and the revealed Word of God.

3. Exercise your own critical thinking. Don't assume that a book is "Christian" because you found it in a Christian bookstore. One of my local Christian bookstores sells the political opinion

books of Rush Limbaugh, the money-making books of Zig Ziglar, and the quasi-spiritual books of Scott Peck. I have seen books that are no more than personal diatribes against Hillary Clinton, tales of near-death experiences, twelve-step recovery programs, positive self-talk strategies, and hate-mongering political invective shelved next to Bible study guides. None of these books contains a shred of true Christianity, even though they are sold by Christian book distributors and are read by many professing Christians.

4. Rely on the ultimate authority of Scripture. Always return to your benchmark, the Word of God, when analyzing a work about Christian living. And if you have been studying the Bible in the way and with the tools discussed earlier in this chapter, you will have no trouble spotting the heresies, distortions, and lies that the enemy insinuates into self-help literature, religious or otherwise.

REMEMBER WHO OUR ENEMY IS

The French poet Charles Baudelaire wrote that the devil's cleverest ploy is to persuade us that he doesn't exist. We need to keep Baudelaire's warning firmly in mind when evaluating self-help materials. Self-help's insistence that our problems and needs are psychological or sociological or even genetic in origin is no more than Satan's attempt to convince us that he doesn't exist and that sin and evil are outmoded constructs from a primitive, superstitious time in human history. But behind the warm and comforting—even the superficially Christian—message of self-help is the creature whom Jesus described in his harshest polemic as "a murderer from the beginning, not holding to the truth, for there is no truth in him. When he lies, he speaks his native language, for he is a liar and the father of lies."[29] The lies of Satan led to Adam's death. The lies of Satan murdered Christ. The lies of Satan in the self-help movement are working today to subvert Christ's church. To resist the seductive messages of self-help, we need to recognize them as lies and to remember where they came from and who our enemy is.

Notes

CHAPTER 1
WHAT IS SELF-HELP? A BIRD'S-EYE VIEW

1. Leslie Kaufman-Rosen with Tessa Namuth, "Getting in Touch with Your Inner President," *Newsweek*, January 16, 1995, p. 72.

2. David Gelman with Margaret Nelson, Elizabeth Roberts, and Niko Price, "A Pocketful of Miracles," *Newsweek*, September 23, 1991, p. 58.

3. Comment made during a television interview with Bernard Goldberg, "Eye to Eye," August 31, 1995.

4. Richard Hofstadter, *Anti-intellectualism in American Life* (New York: Alfred A. Knopf, 1966), p. 25.

5. Robert Wuthnow, "Small Groups Forge New Notions of Community and the Sacred," *The Christian Century*, December 8, 1993, p. 1239.

6. David D. Burns, M.D., *Ten Days to Self-Esteem* (New York: William Morrow & Co., 1993).

7. Gelman, "Pocketful of Miracles," p. 58.

8. Hofstadter, *Anti-intellectualism,* p. 267.

9. Ruth Fishel, *The Journey Within: A Spiritual Path to Recovery* (Deerfield Beach, Fla.: Health Communications, Inc., 1987), p. 47.

10. Michael Brennan, "Self-Indulgent Self-Help," *Newsweek*, January 20, 1992, p. 8.

11. Wuthnow, "Small Groups Forge New Notions," p. 1239.

12. Ben Carson, M.D., *Think Big: Unleashing Your Potential for Excellence* (Grand Rapids, Mich.: Zondervan, 1992), pp. 183-84.

13. Wendy Kaminer, *I'm Dysfunctional, You're Dysfunctional* (Reading, Mass: Addison-Wesley, 1992), p. 120.

14. Barbara Sher, *I Could Do Anything If I Only Knew What It Is* (New York: Delacorte Press, 1994).

15. Peter McWilliams and John-Roger, *Do It! Let's Get Off Our Buts* (Los Angeles: Prelude Press, Inc., 1991).

16. Charles Givens, *SuperSelf: Doubling Your Personal Effectiveness* (New York: Simon & Schuster, 1993).

17. Hofstadter, *Anti-intellectualism,* p. 265.

18. Norman Vincent Peale, *A Guide to Confident Living* (New York: Prentice Hall, 1948), p. 55.

19. Wuthnow, "Small Groups Forge New Notions," pp. 1239-40.

20. Quoted in Doug LeBlanc, "Recovery Books Turn Problems into Bestsellers," *Christianity Today*, September 16, 1991, p. 70.

21. Rick Marin with Susan Miller and Nina A. Biddle, "High-Impact Serenity," *Newsweek*, August 7, 1995, p. 50.

22. Hofstadter, *Anti-intellectualism,* p. 268.

23. Wuthnow, "Small Groups Forge New Notions," p. 1236.

24. Hanna Rosin, "Woolly Pulpit: God, Without the Guilt," *The New Republic*, March 13, 1995, p. 12.

25. Andrew Weil, M.D., *Spontaneous Healing* (New York: Alfred A. Knopf, 1995), p. 122.

CHAPTER 2
HOW DID THE SELF-HELP MOVEMENT BEGIN?

1. Larzer Ziff, *Puritanism in America: New Culture in a New World* (New York: Viking, 1973), p. 15.

2. Ibid., pp. 14-15.

3. Ibid., p. 24.

4. Quoted in Ziff, p. 24.

5. Paul K. Conkin, *Puritans and Pragmatists* (Bloomington, Ind.: Indiana University Press, 1968), p. 11.

6. L. Jesse Lemisch, ed., *Benjamin Franklin: The Autobiography and Other Writings* (New York: The New American Library, 1961), p. 72.

7. Sydney E. Ahlstrom, *A Religious History of the American People* (New Haven, Conn.: Yale University Press, 1972), p. 425.

8. Ibid., p. 591.

9. Ralph Waldo Emerson, *Essays* (New York: A. L. Burt Publisher), p. 33.

10. Quoted in Ahlstrom, p. 601.

11. Quoted in Ahlstrom, p. 1030.

12. Quoted in Ahlstrom, p. 602.

13. Louis B. Wright, "Franklin's Legacy," *Virginia Quarterly Review*, XXII, 1946, p. 268.

14. Quoted in Louis Schneider and Sanford M. Dornbusch, *Popular Religion: Inspirational Books in America* (Chicago: The University of Chicago Press, 1958), p. 16.

15. Ahlstrom, *A Religious History,* p. 1024.

16. Ibid., p. 1051.

17. Richard Hofstadter, *Anti-intellectualism in American Life* (New York: Alfred A. Knopf, 1966), p. 265.

CHAPTER 3
WHAT SUSTAINS THE SELF-HELP MOVEMENT?

1. Steve Salerno, "Possessed!" *The American Legion*, June 1994, p. 32.

2. Ibid., p. 33.

3. Daisy Maryles, "A Decade of Megasellers," *Publishers Weekly*, June 5, 1990, p. 24.

4. Daisy Maryles, "Truth Is Weaker Than Fiction," *Publishers Weekly*, January 6, 1992, p. 83.

5. Daisy Maryles, "Embraced by the List: Bestsellers '94," *Publishers Weekly*, January 2, 1995, p. 50.

6. "Eye to Eye," Bernard Goldberg, reporter, August 31, 1995.

7. Doug LeBlanc, "Recovery Books Turn Problems into Bestsellers," *Christianity Today*, September 16, 1991, p. 70.

8. Jeffrey L. Sheler, "Is God Lost As Sales Rise?" *U.S. News & World Report*, March 13, 1995, p. 63.

9. Os Guinness, *Fit Bodies, Fat Minds* (Grand Rapids, Mich.: Baker Books, 1994), p. 28.

10. Quoted in Guinness, p. 70.

11. Quoted in Irvin G. Wyllie, *The Self-Made Man in America: The Myth of Rags to Riches* (New York: The Free Press, 1954), p. 10.

12. Ibid., p. 174.

13. Ephesians 6:12.

CHAPTER 4
LIE ONE: I BELONG TO MYSELF

1. C. S. Lewis, *The Screwtape Letters*, in *The Best of C. S. Lewis* (Carol Stream, Ill.: Christianity Today, Inc., 1969), pp. 76–77.

2. Matthew 6:21.

3. Abraham H. Maslow, *Toward a Psychology of Being*, 2nd ed. (New York: Van Nostrand Reinhold, 1968), pp. 71–72.

4. Wayne Dyer, *Pulling Your Own Strings: Dynamic Techniques for Confidently Enjoying Your Life, Your Way, Without Being Manipulated* (New York: Thomas Y. Crowell Co., 1978), pp. xv–xvi.

5. Leo Buscaglia, *Personhood: The Art of Being Fully Human* (Thorofare, N.J.: Slack, Inc., 1978), p. 147.

6. Terry Cole-Whittaker, *Love and Power in a World Without Limits: A Woman's Guide to the Goddess Within* (San Francisco: Harper & Row, 1989), p. 17.

7. Ibid., p. xi.

8. John-Roger and Peter McWilliams, *Do It! Let's Get Off Our Buts* (Los Angeles: Prelude Press, 1991), p. 157.

9. Lewis B. Smedes, *Shame and Grace: Healing the Shame We Don't Deserve* (Grand Rapids, Mich: Zondervan, 1993), pp. 76, 144.

10. Francis A. Schaeffer, *Escape from Reason* (Downers Grove, Ill.: InterVarsity Press, 1968), p. 34.

11. Jeffrey B. Abramson, *Liberation and Its Limits: The Moral and Political Thought of Freud* (New York: The Free Press, 1984), p. 2.

12. Barry A. Ellsworth, *Living in Love with Yourself* (Salt Lake City, Utah: Breakthrough Publishing, 1988), p. 143.

13. Ian Kent and William Nicholls, *I AMness: The Discovery of the Self Beyond the Ego* (Indianapolis: The Bobbs-Merrill Company, Inc., 1972), p. 127.

14. Cole-Whittaker, *Love and Power,* p. xiii.

15. M. Scott Peck, *The Road Less Traveled: A New Psychology of Love, Traditional Values and Spiritual Growth* (New York: Simon and Schuster, 1978), p. 269.

16. Irene C. Kassorla, *Go for It! How to Win at Love, Work, and Play* (New York: Delacorte Press, 1984), p. 16.

17. Leo P. Rock, S.J., *Making Friends with Yourself: Christian Growth and Self-Acceptance* (New York: Paulist Press, 1990), p. 6.

18. Dale Hanson Bourke, *You Can Make Your Dreams Come True* (Old Tappan, N.J.: Fleming H. Revell Co., 1985).

19. Muriel James and Dorothy Jongeward, *Born to Win: Transactional Analysis with Gestalt Experiments* (Reading, Mass.: Addison-Wesley, 1973), p. 1.

20. Bobbe Sommer, *Psycho-Cybernetics 2000* (Englewood Cliff, N.J.: Prentice Hall, 1993).

21. Rock, *Making Friends,* p. 10.

22. *The Best of Josh McDowell: A Ready Defense,* comp. Bill Wilson (San Bernardino, Calif.: Here's Life Publishers, 1990), p. 317.

23. Ibid., p. 319.

24. Quoted in *The Best of Josh McDowell,* p. 320.

25. Charles Colson, *Who Speaks for God? Confronting the World with Real Christianity* (Wheaton, Ill.: Crossway Books, 1985), p. 35.

26. Reinhold Niebuhr, *The Nature and Destiny of Man. Vol. 1. Human Nature* (New York: Charles Scribner's Sons, 1941), p. 179.

27. Quoted in Niebuhr, p. 187.

28. Psalm 100:3.

29. John 1:3.

30. 1 Corinthians 6:19-20.

31. Ephesians 1:7-8.

32. Colossians 1:15-16.

33. Daniel 7:13-14 (NAS).

34. Isaiah 16:5.

35. Revelation 11:15.

36. Colson, *Who Speaks for God?* p. 36.

37. 2 Corinthians 12:9.

CHAPTER 5
LIE TWO: I AM ENTITLED TO A LIFE OF HAPPINESS AND FULFILLMENT

1. David G. Myers, *The Pursuit of Happiness: Who Is Happy—and Why* (New York: William Morrow and Co., Inc., 1992), pp. 20-21.

2. Harold H. Bloomfield, *Happiness: The TM Program, Psychiatry, and Enlightenment* (New York: Dawn Press, 1976), p. 14.

3. Alan Epstein, *How to Be Happier Day by Day: A Year of Mindful Actions* (New York, Viking, 1993), p. xi.

4. Richard Carlson, *You Can Be Happy No Matter What* (San Rafael, Calif.: New World Library, 1992), p. xi.

5. Bloomfield, *Happiness,* p. 14.

6. Ibid.

7. Jane Nelson, *Understanding: Eliminating Stress and Finding Serenity in Life and Relationships* (Rocklin, Calif.: Prima Publishing and Communications, 1988), p. 27.

8. Ken Keyes, Jr., *Your Life Is a Gift, So Make the Most of It!* (Coos Bay, Ore.: Love Line Books, 1987), p. 11.

9. John-Roger and Peter McWilliams, *You Can't Afford the Luxury of a Negative Thought* (Los Angeles: Prelude Press, Inc., 1991), p. 205.

10. Bloomfield, *Happiness,* p. 125.

11. Pierre Teilhard de Chardin, *On Love and Happiness* (San Francisco: Harper & Row, 1984), p. 77.

12. Epstein, *How to Be Happier.*

13. Billy Mills, *Wokini: A Lakota Journey to Happiness and Self-Understanding* (New York: Orion Books, 1990), p. 67.

14. Harold Greenwald, *The Happy Person: A Seven-Step Plan* (New York: Stein and Day Publ., 1984).

15. Myers, *The Pursuit of Happiness,* p. 20.

16. Nancy Ashley, *Create Your Own Happiness: A Seth Workbook* (New York: Prentice Hall, 1988).

17. Carlson, *You Can Be Happy,* p. 64 [the author's italics].

18. Mills, *Wokini,* p. 66.

19. Robert Schuller, *The Be (Happy) Attitudes* (Waco, Tex.: Word Books, 1985), pp. 14, 16.

20. McWilliams, *You Can't Afford,* p. 205.

21. Craig S. Keener, *The IVP Bible Background Commentary, New Testament* (Downers Grove, Ill.: InterVarsity Press, 1993), pp. 55-56.

22. Louis Schneider and Sanford M. Dornbusch, *Popular Religion: Inspirational Books in America* (Chicago: The University of Chicago Press, 1958), p. 45.

23. Norman Vincent Peale with Donald T. Kauffman, *Bible Power for Successful Living* (New York: Fleming H. Revell, 1993), p. 52.

24. Carlson, *You Can Be Happy,* p. 138.

25. Robert J. Ringer, *Looking Out for #1* (New York: Fawcett Crest, 1977), p. 17.

26. Zig Ziglar, *Over the Top* (Nashville, Tenn.: Thomas Nelson, 1994), p. 174.

27. "First Person," Maria Shriver, September 6, 1995.

28. Ephesians 2:8-9.

29. Os Guinness, *Fit Bodies, Fat Minds,* p. 46.

30. C. S. Lewis, *The Problem of Pain* (New York: Macmillan Publishing Company, 1962), p. 93.

31. C. S. Lewis, *Letters to Malcolm: Chiefly on Prayer* (New York: Harcourt Brace & Co., 1992), p. 93.

32. Lewis, *The Problem of Pain,* p. 40.

33. Chardin, *On Love and Happiness,* pp. 78-79.

34. Nelson, *Understanding,* pp. 69-70.

35. Lewis, *The Problem of Pain,* p. 115.

36. Zechariah 8:19.

37. Genesis 30:13.

38. Psalm 113:9; 127:5.

39. James 5:13.

40. 2 Corinthians 7:13.

41. Ecclesiastes 2:26.

42. Ecclesiastes 3:13.

43. Ecclesiastes 5:19.

44. Ecclesiastes 7:14.

45. Psalm 68:3.

46. Psalm 128:1-2 (KJV).

47. Ecclesiastes 3:12.

48. Job 5:17.

49. 1 Peter 3:14.

50. 1 Peter 4:14.

51. Numbers 15:39 (KJV).

52. Matthew 6:33.

53. Deuteronomy 4:29.

CHAPTER 6
LIE THREE: I WAS BORN TO GREATNESS

1. Leo Weidner, *Achieving the Balance* (Provo, Utah: LAW Enterprises, 1988).

2. John-Roger and Peter McWilliams, *Do It! Let's Get Off Our Buts* (Los Angeles: Prelude Press, 1991), p. 77.

3. Brian Tracy and Bettie B. Young, *Achievement, Happiness, Popularity and Success* (Solana Beach, Calif.: The Phoenix Educational Foundation, 1988), p. 1.

4. Muriel James and Dorothy Jongeward, *Born to Win: Transactional Analysis with Gestalt Experiments* (Reading, Mass.: Addison-Wesley, 1973), p. 1.

5. Arnold M. Patent, *You Can Have It All* (Hillsboro, Ore.: Beyond Words Publ., 1995), p. 83.

6. Og Mandino, *The Greatest Salesman in the World* (New York: Frederick Fell Publishers, Inc., 1968), p. 71.

7. Irving Oyle and Susan Jean, *The Wizdom Within* (Tiburon, Calif.: H. J. Kramer, Inc., 1992), p. x.

8. Tom Morris, *True Success: A New Philosophy of Excellence* (New York: G. P. Putnam's Sons, 1994), p. 284.

9. Brian Tracy, *Maximum Achievement* (New York: Simon & Schuster, 1993), p. 11.

10. Shad Helmstetter, *What to Say When You Talk to Yourself* (Scottsdale, Ariz.: Grindle Press, 1986), p. 1.

11. Charles R. Swindoll, *Living Above the Level of Mediocrity* (Dallas, Tex.: Word Publishing, 1989), p. 18.

12. Psalm 145:3 (KJV).

13. Philippians 2:9-11.

14. Mark 1:7.

15. Isaiah 53:12.

16. Psalm 51:5.

17. Job 25:4.

18. Job 15:14.

19. Jeremiah 17:9 (KJV).

20. Romans 3:23.

21. Romans 7:14.

22. Romans 6:23.

23. Genesis 2:7.

24. Genesis 3:19.

25. Psalm 144:3.

26. Job 5:7.

27. C. S. Lewis, *The Problem of Pain* (New York: Macmillan Publishing Company, 1962), p. 76.

28. Ibid., pp. 78-79.

CHAPTER 7
LIE FOUR: I CAN BE AS SUCCESSFUL AS I WANT, IF ONLY . . .

1. Irvin G. Wyllie, *The Self-Made Man in America: The Myth of Rags to Riches* (New York: The Free Press, 1954), pp. 3-4.

2. Charles J. Givens, *SuperSelf: Doubling Your Personal Effectiveness* (New York: Simon & Schuster, 1993), p. 12.

3. Helen Gurley Brown, *Having It All* (New York: Simon & Schuster, 1982), p. 428.

4. Terry Cole-Whittaker, *Love and Power in a World Without Limits: A Woman's Guide to the Goddess Within* (San Francisco: Harper & Row, 1989), p. 129.

5. Robert J. Ringer, *Looking Out for #1* (New York: Fawcett Crest, 1977), p. 159.

6. Leo Weidner, *Achieving the Balance* (Provo, Utah: LAW Enterprises, 1988), p. 4.

7. Napoleon Hill, *Think and Grow Rich* (New York: Fawcett Crest, 1960), p. 37.

8. Givens, *SuperSelf,* p. 13.

9. Ringer, *Looking Out for #1*, p. 164.

10. Matthew 6:33.

11. Wyllie, *Self-Made Man*, p. 56.

12. Ibid., p. 172.

13. Mike Murdock, *One-Minute Businessman's Devotional* (Tulsa, Okla.: Honor Books, 1992), pp. 20, 156, 160.

14. Thomas Howard, *C. S. Lewis, Man of Letters: A Reading of His Fiction* (San Francisco: Ignatius Press, 1987), p. 136.

15. Ringer, *Looking Out for #1*, p. 160.

16. C. S. Lewis, *Mere Christianity* (New York: Macmillan Publishing Company, 1952), p. 109.

17. Ibid.

18. Ibid., p. 111.

19. Quoted in Reinhold Niebuhr, *The Nature and Destiny of Man. Vol. 1. Human Nature* (New York: Charles Scribner's Sons, 1941), p. 188.

20. Howard, *C. S. Lewis, Man of Letters,* p. 84.

21. Weidner, *Achieving the Balance,* p. 5.

22. Les Brown, *Live Your Dreams* (New York: William Morrow & Co., Inc., 1992), p. 81.

23. Ibid., pp. 197, 200.

24. Zig Ziglar, *Over the Top* (Nashville, Tenn.: Thomas Nelson, 1994), pp. 100-101.

25. Louis Schneider and Sanford M. Dornbusch, *Popular Religion: Inspirational Books in America* (Chicago: The University of Chicago Press, 1958), p. 51.

26. Os Guinness, *Fit Bodies, Fat Minds* (Grand Rapids, Mich.: Baker Books, 1994), p. 82.

27. Quoted in Schneider and Dornbusch, *Popular Religion,* p. 1.

28. 2 Timothy 3:12.

29. Norman Vincent Peale, *A Guide to Confident Living* (New York: Prentice Hall, 1948), p. 36.

30. Churches Alive, *Alive! God in Intimate Relationship with You* (Colorado Springs, Colo.: NavPress, 1986), p. 9.

31. Murdock, *One-Minute Devotional,* p. 143.

32. Lewis, *Mere Christianity,* p. 111.

33. Craig S. Keener, *The IVP Bible Background Commentary, New Testament* (Downers Grove, Ill.: InterVarsity Press, 1993), p. 91.

34. Lewis, *Mere Christianity,* p. 97.

35. Mark 8:34.

36. Keener, *The IVP Bible Background Commentary,* p. 157.

37. Murdock, *One-Minute Devotional,* p. 43.

38. C. S. Lewis, *The Silver Chair* (New York: Macmillan Publishing Company, 1953), p. 143.

39. Romans 8:17.

40. Philippians 1:29.

41. 1 Peter 4:13.

CHAPTER 8
LIE FIVE: I NEED TO BUILD MY SELF-ESTEEM

1. *Entrepreneur*, May 1995, p. 89.

2. Morton Hunt, "The Secret of Self-Esteem," *Woman's Day*, July 18, 1995.

3. Shirley MacLaine, *Going Within: A Guide for Inner Transformation* (New York: Bantam Books, 1989), p. 27.

4. David A. Seamands, *Freedom from the Performance Trap: Letting Go of the Need to Achieve* (Wheaton, Ill.: Victor Books, 1988), p. 17.

5. David A. Burns, *Ten Days to Self-Esteem* (New York: William Morrow & Co., 1993), p. 189.

6. Joan C. Harvey, *If I'm So Successful, Why Do I Feel Like a Fake?: The Imposter Phenomenon* (New York: St. Martin's Press, 1985), p. 7.

7. Jack Canfield and Harold C. Wells, *100 Ways to Enhance Self-Concept in the Classroom: A Handbook for Parents and Teachers* (New York: Prentice Hall, 1976).

8. Ibid.

9. Reynold Bean, *Honesty, Perseverance and Other Virtues: Using the 4 Conditions of Self-Esteem in Elementary and Middle Schools* (Santa Cruz, Calif.: Education, Training & Research Assoc., 1992).

10. Michael P. Nichols, *No Place to Hide: Facing Shame So We Can Find Self-Respect* (New York: Simon & Schuster, 1991), p. 170.

11. Robert H. Schuller, *Self-Esteem: The New Reformation* (Waco, Tex.: Word Books, 1982), p. 31.

12. Francis A. Schaeffer, *Escape from Reason* (Downers Grove, Ill.: InterVarsity Press, 1968).

13. Francis A. Schaeffer, *Death in the City* (Downers Grove, Ill.: InterVarsity Press, 1969), pp. 79-80.

14. Schuller, *Self-Esteem*, p. 34.

15. *Building Self-Esteem: Realities of Human Behavior,* (Barksdale Foundation, 1991).

16. Schuller, *Self-Esteem,* pp. 14-15.

17. Lewis B. Smedes, *Shame and Grace: Healing the Shame We Don't Deserve* (Grand Rapids, Mich.: Zondervan, 1993), p. 55.

18. Ibid., p. 122.

19. Luke 15:21.

20. Kenneth L. Woodward, "What Ever Happened to Sin?" *Newsweek*, February 6, 1995, p. 23.

21. Schuller, *Self-Esteem*, p. 138.

22. Ibid., p. 127.

23. Quoted in Steve Salerno, "Possessed!" *American Legion*, June 1994, p. 65.

24. Quoted in Douglas Wilson, *Recovering the Lost Tools of Learning* (Wheaton, Ill.: Crossway Books, 1991), p. 15.

25. Ibid., p. 15.

26. Richard Hofstadter, *Anti-intellectualism in American Life* (New York: Alfred A. Knopf, 1966), p. 269.

27. Quoted in Jonathan Alter and Pat Wingert, "The Return of Shame," *Newsweek*, February 6, 1995, p. 22.

28. "CT Talks to Alan Loy McGinnis," *Christianity Today*, February 5, 1988, p. 55.

29. Bruce Davis, *The Magical Child Within You* (Berkeley, Calif.: Celestial Arts, 1985), p. 39.

30. Roy F. Baumeister, *Escaping the Self* (New York: Basic Books, 1991), p. 179.

31. Burns, *Ten Days to Self-Esteem*, p. 188.

32. Nichols, *No Place to Hide*, p. 169.

33. Earl Wilson, *The Discovered Self: The Search for Self-Acceptance* (Downers Grove, Ill.: InterVarsity Press, 1985).

34. Harold Kushner, *Who Needs God?* (New York: Summit Books, 1989), p. 198.

35. Schuller, *Self-Esteem*.

36. Leo Buscaglia, *Personhood: The Art of Being Fully Human* (Thorofare, N.J.: Slack, Inc., 1978), p. 102.

37. Bruce Davis, *Magical Child*, p. 75.

38. Leviticus 19:18; Matthew 22:39.

39. Romans 12:10.

40. Philippians 2:3.

41. John 15:13.

42. Nathaniel Branden, *The Six Pillars of Self-Esteem* (New York: Bantam Books, 1994).

43. Deuteronomy 5:15.

44. Matthew 18:4.

45. Galatians 6:14.

46. Romans 12:3; Galatians 5:26; Colossians 3:12.

47. James 1:9; 4:10.

48. Genesis 18:27.

49. Genesis 32:10.

50. Exodus 3:11.

51. 2 Samuel 7:18.

52. Psalm 8.

53. Isaiah 66:2; Leviticus 26:9.

CHAPTER 9
LIE SIX: I NEED TO LEARN POSITIVE SELF-TALK

1. Shad Helmstetter, *What to Say When You Talk to Yourself* (Scottsdale, Ariz.: Grindle Press, 1986).

2. Douglas Wilson, *Recovering the Lost Tools of Learning* (Wheaton, Ill.: Crossway Books, 1991).

3. David G. Myers, *The Pursuit of Happiness: Who Is Happy—and Why* (New York: William Morrow and Co., Inc., 1992), p. 26.

4. Ronald Inglehart, *Culture Shift in Advanced Industrialized Society* (Princeton: Princeton University Press, 1990).

5. Hubert L. Dreyfus, *What Computers Still Can't Do: A Critique of Artificial Reason* (Cambridge: The MIT Press, 1993).

6. Churches Alive, *Alive! God in Intimate Relationship with You* (Colorado Springs, Colo.: NavPress, 1986), p. 7.

7. Ira Progoff, *At a Journal Workshop* (New York: Dialogue House Library, 1975), p. 9.

8. Ibid., p. 160.

9. C. S. Lewis, *Surprised by Joy: The Shape of My Early Life* (New York: Harcourt Brace & Company, 1984).

10. Dietrich Bonhoeffer, *The Cost of Discipleship* (New York: Macmillan Publishing Company, 1959), p. 97.

11. Myers, *Pursuit of Happiness,* p. 88.

12. Walter Elwell, ed., *Evangelical Commentary on the Bible* (Grand Rapids, Mich.: Baker Book House, 1989), p. 424.

13. Ibid., p. 425.

14. Winfried Corduan, *Reasonable Faith: Basic Christian Apologetics* (Nashville, Tenn.: Broadman & Holman, 1993), p. 33.

15. Irving Oyle and Susan Jean, *The Wizdom Within: On Daydreams, Realities, and Revelations* (Tiburon, Calif.: H. J. Kramer, 1992), p. 26.

16. Ibid., pp. 36, 38.

17. Ibid., p. 26.

18. Ibid.
19. Helmstetter, *What to Say,* p. 67.
20. Colin Brown, *Christianity & Western Thought,* Vol. 1 (Downers Grove, Ill.: InterVarsity Press, 1990), p. 80.
21. Harold Bloom, *The American Religion: The Emergence of the Post-Christian Nation* (New York: Simon & Schuster, 1992).
22. Matthew 13:9.
23. John 10:27.
24. John 18:37b.
25. Acts 10:44.
26. Psalm 85:8.
27. Deuteronomy 4:36.
28. Ecclesiastes 7:5.

CHAPTER 10
THE SELF-HELP MOVEMENT AS A RELIGION

1. Richard Hofstadter, *Anti-intellectualism in American Life* (New York: Alfred A. Knopf, 1966), p. 255.
2. David A. Burns, *Ten Days to Self-Esteem* (New York: William Morrow & Co., 1993), p. 10.
3. Leo Weidner, *Achieving the Balance* (Provo, Utah: LAW Enterprises, 1988), p. 4.
4. James 2:17, 26.
5. Erica E. Goode, "Human Potential Hits 30," *U.S. News & World Report,* June 29, 1992, p. 69.
6. Romans 8:26.
7. Mike Murdock, *One-Minute Businessman's Devotional* (Tulsa, Okla.: Honor Books, 1992), p. 222.
8. Os Guinness, *Fit Bodies, Fat Minds* (Grand Rapids, Mich.: Baker Books, 1994), p. 88.
9. Rick Marin, "High-Impact Serenity," *Newsweek,* August 7, 1995, p. 50.
10. Ezekiel 23.
11. Harold Bloom, *The American Religion: The Emergence of the Post-Christian Nation* (New York: Simon & Schuster, 1992), p. 23.
12. Quoted in Marin, p. 50.

CHAPTER 11
LIFE BEHIND ENEMY LINES

1. David F. Wells, *God in the Wasteland* (Grand Rapids, Mich.: Eerdmans Publishing Company, 1994), p. 68.

2. David F. Wells, *No Place for Truth* (Grand Rapids, Mich.: Eerdmans Publishing Company, 1993), p. 290.

3. Os Guinness, *Dining with the Devil: The Megachurch Movement Flirts with Modernity* (Grand Rapids, Mich.: Baker Book House, 1993), p. 84.

4. Ibid., p. 49.

5. Ibid., p. 58.

6. Wells, *God in the Wasteland,* p. 67.

7. Robert Wuthnow, "How Small Groups Are Transforming Our Lives," *Christianity Today,* February 7, 1994, p. 23.

8. Quoted in John W. Kennedy, "Redeeming the Wasteland?" *Christianity Today,* October 2, 1995, p. 93.

9. Malachi 3:10.

10. Quoted in Kenneth L. Woodward, "Do We Need Satan?" *Newsweek,* November 13, 1995, p. 67.

11. Quoted in Kennedy, p. 100.

12. Tim Stafford, "The Therapeutic Revolution: How Christian Counseling Is Changing the Church," *Christianity Today,* May 17, 1993, p. 32.

13. Warren Bird, "The Great Small Group Takeover," *Christianity Today,* February 7, 1994, p. 25.

14. Robert Wuthnow, "Small Groups," p. 23.

15. Warren Bird, "Small Group Takeover," p. 29.

16. Ibid.

17. Wuthnow, "Small Groups," p. 22.

18. Susan Cyre, "Fallout Escalates Over 'Goddess' Sophia Worship," *Christianity Today,* April 4, 1994, p. 74.

19. C. S. Lewis, *The Pilgrim's Regress* (Grand Rapids, Mich.: Eerdmans Publishing Company, 1981 edition), pp. 179-80.

20. James Hunter, *American Evangelicalism* (New Brunswick, N.J.: Rutgers University Press, 1983), pp. 94-98.

21. Quoted in Jeffrey L. Sheler, "Is God Lost As Sales Rise?" *U.S. News & World Report,* March 13, 1995, p. 63.

22. Howard A. Snyder, "Is God's Love Unconditional?" *Christianity Today,* July 17, 1995, p. 30.

23. Andrew Peyton Thomas, "Can We Ever Go Back?" *The Wall Street Journal,* August 9, 1995, p. A8.

24. Dietrich Bonhoeffer, *The Cost of Discipleship* (New York: Macmillan Publishing Company, 1959), p. 99.

25. Ibid., p. 97.

26. Lewis B. Smedes, *Shame and Grace: Healing the Shame We Don't Deserve* (Grand Rapids, Mich.: Zondervan, 1993), p. 81.

27. Quoted in Clyde S. Kilby, *The Christian World of C. S. Lewis* (Grand Rapids, Mich.: Eerdmans Publishing Company, 1964), p. 158.

28. Bonhoeffer, *Cost of Discipleship,* p. 45.

29. Ibid., p. 54.

CHAPTER 12
WITHSTANDING THE ENEMY'S LIES

1. 2 Timothy 3:16-17.

2. Matthew 22:29-33.

3. Quoted in Karen R. Long, "Bible Knowledge at Record Low, Pollster Says," *National Catholic Reporter,* July 15, 1994, p. 9.

4. Thomas Ehrlich, "The Bible: Our Heritage," *The Saturday Evening Post,* May/June 1991, p. 66.

5. Earl D. Wilson, *The Discovered Self: The Search for Self-Acceptance* (Downers Grove, Ill.: InterVarsity Press, 1985), p. 19.

6. Mike Murdock, *One-Minute Businessman's Devotional* (Tulsa, Okla.: Honor Books, 1992).

7. Robert J. Wicks, *Touching the Holy: Ordinariness, Self-Esteem, and Friendship* (Notre Dame, Ind.: Ave Maria Press, 1992), p. 9.

8. Quoted in G. Walter Hansen, "Words from God's Heart," *Christianity Today,* October 23, 1995, p. 23.

9. Ibid., p. 25.

10. Walt Russell, "What It Means to Me," *Christianity Today,* October 26, 1992, pp. 30-31 [my emphasis].

11. Ibid., p. 30.

12. Ibid., p. 31 [the author's emphasis].

13. Quoted in "Classic and Contemporary Excerpts," *Christianity Today,* October 25, 1993, p. 73.

14. Walt Russell, "What It Means to Me," p. 32.

15. Jack P. Lewis, *The English Bible from KJV to NIV: A History and Evaluation* (Grand Rapids, Mich.: Baker Book House, 1981), p. 366.

16. Quoted in *Christianity Today*, October 25, 1993, p. 73.

17. Timothy George, "What We Mean When We Say It's True," *Christianity Today,* October 23, 1995, p. 19.

18. Ecclesiastes 1:9.

19. William Barclay, *The Apostles' Creed for Everyman* (New York: Harper & Row, 1967), p. 10.

20. *The Book of Common Prayer* (New York: The Seabury Press, 1977), p. 846.

21. Hebrews 10:24-25. See also Craig S. Keener, *The IVP Bible Background Commentary, New Testament* (Downers Grove, Ill.: InterVarsity Press, 1993), pp. 670-71.

22. Colin Brown, *Christianity & Western Thought*, Vol. 1 (Downers Grove, Ill.: InterVarsity Press, 1990), p. 99.

23. Hebrews 11:1 (KJV).

24. Winfried Corduan, *Reasonable Faith: Basic Christian Apologetics* (Nashville, Tenn.: Broadman & Holman, 1993), p. 21.

25. Ibid., p. 22.

26. C. S. Lewis, *Letters to Malcolm: Chiefly on Prayer* (New York: Harcourt Brace & Co., 1992), p. 76.

27. Matthew 20:16.

28. Matthew 10:39.

29. John 8:44.

Suggested Readings

The following books are not specifically about any aspects of the self-help movement. Rather, they all contain ideas that are inimical to self-help because they promote orthodox Christianity, they encourage critical thought, they further the life of the mind, and they foster a worldview that takes us outside our parochial interests and away from a relentless focus on the self. I believe that reading books such as these helps us see through the thin veneer of self-help truths to the core of self-help lies.

DIETRICH BONHOEFFER

The Cost of Discipleship. New York: Macmillan Publishing Company, 1959.

COLIN BROWN

Christianity & Western Thought: A History of Philosophers, Ideas & Movements. Downers Grove, Ill.: InterVarsity Press, 1990.

TIM DOWLEY, ORGANIZING EDITOR

Eerdmans' Handbook to the History of Christianity. Grand Rapids, Mich.: Wm. B. Eerdmans Publishing Co., 1977.

OS GUINNESS

Dining with the Devil: The Megachurch Movement Flirts with Modernity. Grand Rapids, Mich.: Baker Book House, 1993.

Fit Bodies, Fat Minds: Why Evangelicals Don't Think and What to Do About It. Grand Rapids, Mich.: Baker Book House, 1994.

C. S. LEWIS

The Great Divorce. New York: Macmillan Paperback, 1963.

Letters to Malcolm: Chiefly on Prayer. New York: HBJ Paperback, 1975.

Mere Christianity. New York: Macmillan Paperback, 1960.

The Problem of Pain. New York: Macmillan Paperback, 1962.

The Screwtape Letters. New York: Macmillan Paperback, 1959.

Surprised by Joy: The Shape of My Early Life. New York: Harcourt Brace & Company, 1984.

The Weight of Glory and Other Addresses. Grand Rapids: Wm. B. Eerdmans Publishing Co., 1965.

MARK A. NOLL

The Scandal of the Evangelical Mind. Grand Rapids: Wm. B. Eerdmans Publishing Co., 1994.

FRANCIS A. SCHAEFFER

Death in the City. Downers Grove, Ill.: InterVarsity Press, 1969.

Escape from Reason. Downers Grove, Ill.: InterVarsity Press, 1968.

The God Who Is There. Downers Grove, Ill.: InterVarsity Press, 1968.

Letters of Francis Schaeffer. Wheaton, Ill.: Crossway Books, 1985.

DAVID F. WELLS

God in the Wasteland: The Reality of Truth in a World of Fading Dreams. Grand Rapids: Wm. B. Eerdmans Publishing Co., 1994.

No Place for Truth or Whatever Happened to Evangelical Theology? Grand Rapids: Wm. B. Eerdmans Publishing Co., 1993.

JOHN D. WOODBRIDGE, GENERAL EDITOR

Great Leaders of the Christian Church. Chicago: Moody Press, 1988.

The following books, while secular in content, are nevertheless useful as background texts for studies of philosophical trends and their influence on contemporary thought, including Christianity and self-help.

ANNE FREMANTLE ET AL.

The Great Ages of Western Philosophy. Boston: Houghton Mifflin Co., 1962.

ANTHONY KENNY, EDITOR

The Oxford History of Western Philosophy. New York: Oxford University Press, 1994.

R. J. HOLLINGDALE

Western Philosophy, an Introduction. New York: Taplinger Publishing Co., Inc., 1979.

Index